STUDIES IN BIBLICAL AND CUNEIFORM LAW

CAHIERS DE LA REVUE BIBLIQUE

26

STUDIES IN BIBLICAL AND CUNEIFORM LAW

PAR

Raymond WESTBROOK
Lecturer in Biblical Law,
The Hebrew University of Jerusalem

PARIS
J. GABALDA et Cie, Éditeurs
RUE PIERRE ET MARIE CURIE, 18
—
1988

PREFACE

Most of the material for this book was compiled as part of a research project on the Biblical Law of Obligations in which I am engaged on behalf of the Institute for Research in Jewish Law of the Hebrew University Faculty of Law. These studies therefore represent only the first tentative step in a vast subject which will take many years to encompass. I am grateful to the Institute and its director, Professor M. Rabello, and also to the Faculty of Law for the resources placed at my disposal in the furtherance of this project.

It is my pleasant duty to thank the fathers of the École Biblique in Jerusalem for giving me the opportunity to publish these studies in their monograph series and for making available to me the facilities of their magnificent library. My thanks are due in particular to my friend and colleague, Marcel Sigrist, without whose inspiration, assistance and constant encouragement, the publication of this book would not have been possible.

Parts of the draft manuscript were read by Dr. T. Frymer-Kensky and Dr. P. Segal, who made many useful comments and criticisms. Responsibility, as usual, remains with the author.

Finally, I wish to thank the typists, Ms. Anne Moss and Ms. Davida Chazan for their work in preparing the manuscript for publication, a task which involved overcoming numerous technical difficulties.

Jerusalem,
December, 1986

ABBREVIATIONS

The following abbreviations have been used for the cuneiform lawcodes:

CU	Codex Ur-Nammu
CU (Yildiz)	Fragment of Codex Ur-Nammu edited by F. Yildiz, *Orientalia* 50 (1981) 87-97.
CL	Codex Lipit-Ishtar
CL (Civil)	Fragment attributed to Codex Lipit-Ishtar, edited by M. Civil, *AS* 16 (1965) 1-12.
CE	Codex Eshnunna
CE (Haddad)	Fragment of Codex Eshnunna (Haddad 116), edited by F.N.H. Al-Rawi, *Sumer* 38 (1982) 117-120.
CH	Codex Hammurabi
AL	Middle) Assyrian Laws
HL	Hittite Laws

The abbreviations used for other cuneiform texts are those of the Chicago Assyrian Dictionary.

TABLE OF CONTENTS

INTRODUCTION

The premise on which these studies are based is that the law of ancient Israel was an integral part of a much wider legal tradition. The different sources in the Bible react to this tradition in a variety of ways, ranging from approval to outright condemnation, but even where their attitude is at its most negative they continue to share its basic concepts and assumptions.

The tradition in question covered the area of the Ancient Near East where cuneiform writing and learning prevailed, but its influence was felt even beyond these bounds. In non-cuneiform script it is to be found not only in the Bible, which at least derives from an area within the cuneiform sphere, but also in the earliest Roman Law.[1]

While the legal systems of the individual societies within this sphere drew upon this tradition, their exact relationship to it (and therefore to each other) is not clear. Were they separate systems derived from a common ancestor, like modern English and American law, or were they the result of the reception of one dominant system by its neighbours and successors, as with the modern Continental systems derived from Roman Law? All we can say is that the connection is definitely not coincidental : the common elements that can be identified in the different systems go far beyond what might be assumed to be an inevitable similarity in the problems facing societies with the same economic and social structure and their solutions thereto. At all events the question is only part of the much wider one of the relationship between the civilizations of the Ancient Near East, since law does not exist in a vacuum.

The common legal tradition finds expression in the sources in many ways. We may mention two which are germane to the contents of this book: legal institutions and the intellectual activity surrounding the law.[2]

---

1 "The Ancient Near Eastern Origins of Roman Law" was the title of a paper given by us to the Société Internationale des Droits de l'Antiquité at Namur in 1985. The thesis was that Roman law was one of the systems on the periphery which was influenced by Ancient Near Eastern Law.

It would be logical to suppose that the Greeks acted as a conduit, but the connection of the earliest Greek code, the Laws of Gortyn, remains unclear. (There are problems of content and dating which cannot be entered into here).

The relationship of Egyptian law to the cuneiform systems is likewise problematic, as is the whole question of outside influences on Egypt. For the purposes of this study it has been assumed that Egyptian Law is not part of the tradition, although this is certainly something of a distortion and may in the light of future research prove to be unfounded.

2 There is also, for example, the Formulae in legal documents. See J.Muffs, *Studies in the Aramaic Legal Papyri from Elephantine*, SDIOAP 8, Leiden 1969.

The legal institution that we shall touch upon is that of kingship. We shall see that there was a common conception of the ideal role of the king in the administration of justice and in his relationship to the traditional rules of law as applied by officials and the courts.

Intellectual activity surrounding the law takes several forms. Firstly, there is the compiling of manuals for the use of priests on matters falling within their competence, such as the rituals to be employed on certain occasions. Examples are found in Babylonia,[3] among the Hittites,[4] and in the legal sections of Leviticus and Numbers.

Secondly, and far more important for our purposes, there are the law codes. The seven codes known to us from the cuneiform sources,[5] the two from the Bible,[6] and the earliest Roman code,[7] are all immediately recognizable as belonging to a single literary genre.[8] Here at least, the connection between them is clear, and we may pause to consider the nature of these texts and the reason for their proliferation.

Recent reseach has shown that these codes are, in origin at least, scientific treatises on the law.[9] They derive from the realm of Mesopotamian science, where similar treatises are to be found on subjects such as divination and on medicine. This form of scientific treatise, presumably invented by the Sumerians, was carried via the Babylonians to every corner of the Near East where cuneiform writing penetrated. In the second millenium their language, Akkadian, was the medium of international diplomacy, commerce and law. Scribal schools were established to teach the language and its cuneiform script to local scribes as far afield as Egypt and

---

3 E.g. Šurpu (ed. E. Reiner AfO Beiheft 11, Graz 1958)

4 See e.g. the material collected by E. Neu in *Althethitische Ritualtexte in Umschrift* StBoT 25 (1980) + 26 (1983). Analogous are the instructions to Temple officials, etc. (ed. E. von Schuler, AfO Beiheft 10, Graz 1957)

5 Codex Ur-Nammu (CU), Codex Lipit-Ishtar (CL), Codex Eshnunna (CE), Codex Hammurabi (CH), Assyrian Laws (AL), Hittite Laws (HL), Neo-Babylonian Laws (NBL)

6 The legal corpus of the Covenant Code (Ex 21,2 - 22,6) and of Deuteronomy (Dt. 21,1 - 25,11)

7 The Twelve Tables (ed. S. Riccobono, *Fontes Iuris Romani Anteiustiniani* Pt 1, Florence 1941, Cap. 2). Like the Bible, the code has come down to us by tradition and not from contemporary sources. In fact, only fragments remain, which have been gleaned from scattered references and quotations in the classical and post-classical legal literature. The present order of the texts is the work of modern scholars. According to tradition, the Twelve Tables were promulgated in 450 B.C.E.

8 See note 9 below.

9 Especially the seminal works of F.R. Kraus ("Ein zentrales Problem des altmesopotamischen Rechtes: Was ist der Codex Hammurabi?", *Genava* 8 (1960) 283-296) and J. Bottéro, ("Le 'Code' de Hammurabi", *Annali della Scuola Normale Superiore de Pisa* 12 (1982) 409-444). For the development and application of the codes, see Westbrook, "Biblical and Cuneiform Law Codes" *RB* 92 (1985) 247-264.

Anatolia. But such scribal schools were more than mere crammers in the art of writing; they may truly be described as the universities of the Ancient Near East. Within their walls literary works were preserved, developed and created, and scientific research pursued.[10] With the spread of the schools, therefore, came the spread of scientific learning. Codex Hammurabi was copied as part of the school curriculum[11] and it is thus not surprising that the local scribes should have developed a legal science for their own systems on the Babylonian model.

As for the specific biblical connection, it should be noted that Babylonian scribal schools were well established in Canaanite cities such as Hatzor and Megiddo prior to the Israelite conquest. No Canaanite law codes have been discovered to date, but legal documents have been found at such sites written not in the local language but in Akkadian.[12] In other words, Akkadian was accepted in these societies as the language of lawyers.

The Mesopotamian scientific treatises employ an approach that is entirely foreign to us. In appearance they are lists of examples, each in the form of a hypothetical set of circumstances and their consequence: "if the circumstances are X, the prediction/disease/judgment is Y." The reason is that Mesopotamian science lacked analytical tools.[13]

Modern scientific method, derived from Greek philosophy, is a vertical system. The material is first organized into general categories, the terminology of these categories defined so that it can at once be seen what material is included and what excluded, then the general categories broken down into successively smaller categories, with appropriate definition of the terminology, until the individual case is reached.

All this was beyond the reach of Mesopotamian science. It was incapable of creating general categories or of defining terms. Consequently it was forced to proceed horizontally, to present concrete examples of the topic under discussion, and to exhaust that topic by the cumulation of ever more examples pertaining to different facets thereof. The result is an extremely fragmentary picture, since an infinite number of examples would be necessary to cover the whole of any given topic. In an attempt to overcome this limitation, the science developed certain techniques. These can be illustrated by the method whereby the law codes were constructed.

10 For an account of the scribes' scientific and literary activities, see A.L. Oppenheim *Ancient Mesopotamia*, Chicago 1964, 243-256, 272-275.

11 See Westbrook, op. cit. note 9 above p. 253 and the literature cited in n. 31 therein.

12 W.W. Hallo and H. Tadmor, "A Lawsuit from Hazor" *IEJ* 27 (1977) 1-11.

13 See Bottéro (op. cit note 9 above) 427-429, 431-435, whose analysis we follow. Our only reservation is that we do not agree that the law codes include practically impossible examples for the sake of completeness, as do the omen-lists.

The starting point was a judgment in an individual case. Preferably a borderline case was taken, since the law in the ordinary case could also be derived from it by implication. For example, in a discussion of rape, a case involving a girl who was betrothed but not married would theoretically inform one also of the position of a fully married woman. The facts and the judgment were then re-cast in the anonymous, objective form of the casuistic sentence that is the hallmark of the Mesopotamian scientific style: "If a man rapes a betrothed woman, his punishment is Y".[14]

That hypothetical question can then be examined more deeply by the technique of variation. Firstly the circumstances can be changed in some details: if the girl were willing, if she were unwilling but unable to call for help, etc., or a vital circumstance can be changed that reverses the judgment from liability to non-liability, or vice-versa.

Secondly, a further set of variations that follow a set pattern may be imposed, such as attributing different grades of status to the parties. This technique, as we shall see in Chapter Two, allows a certain economy in variation: if the variation in circumstances is A,B and the variation in grade 1,2,3, there is no need to give all the possible examples, i.e. A1, A2, A3,,B1, B2, B3. Instead the Code selects for example A2, B1, B3, leaving he reader to fill in the gaps by logical deduction.

The examples that constitute the law codes were not, therefore, cumulated at random, but result from the application of a scientific method. The basic building blocks were "schools problems" - a case that may have begun life as a cause célèbre but then became the object of a theoretical discussion in which all manner of hypothetical variations to the actual circumstances were considered so as to build up a series of precedents grouped around a single theme. These problems were not re-discovered by each legal system but form a canon that was handed on from one system to another through the scientific tradition.

The system nonetheless remained flawed, for in spite of the techniques employed it was not possible to achieve anything near comprehensive discussion of a topic. In practice, logical deduction alone is insufficient to fill in the gaps between examples given ostensibly as markers; some knowledge of the common law[15] is necessary. And indeed, comprehensive treatment in the modern

---

14 For the detailed steps in this construction, see Westbrook, op. cit. note 9 above, 258-264.

15'Common law' is a technical term meaning the traditional corpus of law in a legal system that has been built up from accepted custom and the use of judgments as precedents; as distinguished from law derived from legislation or similar interventions from above. Common law always originates as unwritten law but may then be consigned to writing. It is also to be distinguished from the "Common Law", which refers to systems based on the English legal tradition (as opposed to the Continental).

sense may not have been the aim of the codes, since they assume in the reader a thorough knowledge of the common law. Often where two codes contain the same case, one will omit some detail which the modern reader would have thought necessary. As we shall see, the examples are presented by the codes not as neutral statements in a vacuum but often in order to emphasize a particular point of law. The example is then no more than a vehicle for demonstrating the policy of the law by way of allusion to facts already known to the contemporary reader. This is the closest that the codes can come to enunciating legal principles.

The realization that the law codes are part of a native scientific tradition has important methodological implications for our use of them as sources:

1. As they were aimed at contemporaries and not historians, the codes assume more knowledge than they reveal. To discover the central features of the ancient law, therefore, we must not take the provisions of the codes at their face value, but reconstruct the assumed knowledge. The basis for this reconstruction - apart from the provisions themselves - should be the civilization that forms the framework for the code, its institutions and ideas, whether from legal or non-legal sources. We should not assume the whole paraphernalia of a modern legal system and interpret the code in their light.

2. The law codes are descriptive and not prescriptive. They are not legislation in the modern sense, and it is pointless to attribute to them the incidents of legislation, such as reforms in the law or citation in law-suits. They are essentially a record of the common law, that is the traditional corpus of unwritten law built up mostly through precedents, together with the occasional intervention of administrative measures. On the other hand, it is important to note that they are not a neutral description; there is an attempt to elucidate principles, which in turn demonstrates a concern for certain ideals of justice.

3. The fragmentary presentation of the codes and their attempts to overcome this limitation affects the use of arguments from silence. Such arguments may be of two kinds: negative or positive.

Negative arguments from silence have been used in this field especially by biblical scholars.[16] Their reasoning is firstly that

---

16 Cf. for example M. Greenberg : "...the leniency of biblical law in dealing with all types of property offenses is astonishing. No property offense is punishable with death" ("Some Postulates of Biblical Criminal Law" *Yehezkel Kaufmann Jubilee Volume*, Jerusalem 1960, p. 18); and J.J. Finkelstein: "... the biblical prescription requiring that the ox that had gored a person to death be stoned emerges as the salient feature of the judicial procedure. In this it stands in sharpest contrast with the treatment of the theme in the cuneiform sources, where the fate of the ox merits no judicial attention whatever". (*The Ox That Gored*, Transactions of the American Philosphical Society, Vol. 71 Pt. 2, 1981, p. 29.)

where a rule, or a part thereof, is present in one code but absent in another, the omission is evidence that it was absent from that legal system, or even condemned by it. Secondly, even within the same code, where one paragraph contains a certain element and another paragraph with an analogous rule omits it, that element can be assumed to exist only in the first rule, as opposed to the second.

We would reject this reasoning: indeed, we would argue that the contrary is true. As to the first instance, the schools problems discussed by the codes are multi-faceted. It is seldom that a single code manages to cover every single aspect of the traditional problem; instead each selects such facets as it deems necessary to its own discussion. The rest are not consigned to oblivion; they are part of the common law and their existence is assumed. To take an example from the law of adultery, just some of the facets of the problem dealt with by a plethora of provisions in the law-codes are: 1) adultery by a wife, 2) adultery by a fiancée 3) rape of a wife 4) rape of a fiancée 5) seduction by a wife, the paramour being ignorant of her status.

CU covers cases 4 and 5, CE cases 1 and 4, CH cases 1,2 and 3, AL 1, 3 and 5, and Deuteronomy 1,2 and 4. None of the codes deals with all five cases. It is not to be supposed that the missing cases in each code were not treated by the legal system or if they were that the result was any different from those systems where it does appear in the law code, unless there is positive evidence to the contrary.

On a more specific point HL 197 contains an evidentiary test of rape or adultery for a married woman: in the hills it is taken to be rape; in the town, adultery. Dt 22, 23-27 has the same test but for a fiancée, and adds the further distinction of a fiancée in town who cried for help and one who did not. As the ability to call for help is the obvious rationale behind the test, it is not reasonable to assume that this further distinction did not exist in Hittite law simply because it was not included in the code, or for that matter to suggest that the evidentiary test did not apply to fiancées in Hittite law or to married women in biblical law. It is therefore by combining the partial discussion in each of the separate codes that we are able to reconstruct the complete original problem, and we are entitled to assume prima facie that all the rules of the reconstructed problem applied in each of the systems that have contributed to it. This we would call a positive argument from silence. Of course, it is not inevitable that all the contributing systems slavishly adopted every rule in identical detail, and the assumption would always cede to evidence to the contrary. But that is an argument from evidence, not from silence.

The second instance is a trifle more complicated. We shall argue in the course of this book that in certain circumstances the common law offered the plaintiff two alternative courses of action. The relevant paragraphs of the codes are reacting to this common law rule and according to the point that it wishes to make a paragraph will concentrate on one alternative or the other, but always with the assumption that the other still exists. Only rarely is the full alternative spelled out, most often in sources outside the codes, and we would argue that these sources can be applied to fill the gaps left by the silence of individual paragraphs of the codes. This, then, is another positive argument from silence, but examples of this complex question would best await the full discussion in Chapters Two, Three and Four.

The realization that the biblical codes have their origins in the Mesopotamian scientific tradition likewise has implications for their use as a source:

1. The classic methods of biblical criticism for identifying the sources of narrative passages and dating them certainly remain applicable when comparing the different codes, but not for comparing the individual rules within a single code or the individual parts of a single rule. The evidence from the Ancient Near Eastern law codes is of a very conservative tradition stretching over thousands of years, with age-old rules being reformulated, but remaining in substance the same. Difficulties in the interpretation of a verse in a biblical law code should not therefore be ascribed to amendment or interpolation, as if it were a legislative provision. Nor, since laws have to make sense, should apparent conflicts between verses be ascribed to different sources that incomplete editing has failed to reconcile, as does happen in the narratives.

2. Post-biblical Jewish legal sources cannot be relied upon to fill the gaps in the biblical codes. The sources of positive law, such as the Mishna, represent a development in that they apply a method of legal analysis more akin to our own, dividing the whole of a topic into categories and defining the terms of each. It is true that the Mishna still contains a great deal of casuistic reasoning, as does modern jurisprudence, but it is subordinate to the legal analysis.

The same applies to exegetical works on the biblical codes, such as the Mekhilta. Besides the fact that the exegesis is designed to serve the purposes of a working legal system, not of historical research, the Mekhilta looks at the earlier sources with the same spectacles, coloured by the analytical approach, as the Mishna.

Although these sources certainly contain many older traditions, therefore, it is difficult to distinguish them from later developments. The only criterion, in fact, is whether the same rule already appears in one of the pre-biblical cuneiform sources.

3. In summary, we would argue that biblical law is not to be treated as an autarchic system to which occasional obvious parallels (to modern eyes) may be adduced from the cuneiform

sources.[17] Our approach is a holistic one : to reconstruct the legal problem from all the sources available, among which the biblical sources rank *pari passu*, and only when the rules relating to a particular topic are understood, not least because they form a logical and internally consistent unit, to consider how far the biblical attitude to the problem differs from that of other systems. In this way the biblical sources may be seen to contribute to the understanding of cuneiform law as much as vice-versa.

Finally, a word about the content of this book. The following chapters are a series of connected studies concerning the redress of wrongs in law. In terms of modern law, they are hard to classify: the first chapter might be thought to deal with administrative law or with Equity, while the subsequent chapters could be assigned to criminal law or to delict.

These difficulties arise because the categories of modern legal systems are not applicable to ancient law. Firstly, there was no division of powers as there is in a modern constitution : the executive and the judiciary were regarded as the same power and were to be found in the hands of a single official, whether king, chamberlain, or judge in a local court.

Secondly, the modern division into civil and criminal law, with its separate courts and rules of procedure and evidence, not to mention legal philosophy, had no reflection in the ancient system. As we shall see, their method of redress for wrongs that might nowadays be classed sometimes as criminal and sometimes as civil was based on a completely different concept of the role of the legal system.

17 And by the same token, any apparent differences seized upon as evidence of ideological conflict.

CHAPTER ONE: THE ABUSE OF POWER

A. INTRODUCTION

"You shall not respect persons" says the Book of Deuteronomy[1] in its instructions to the judges, and this principle remains a cornerstone of modern legal systems no less than of ancient. In practice, however, the law does tend to discriminate in favour of the powerful, according them an advantage over their weaker opponents in two different ways.

Firstly, the very fact that the law purports to disregard the relative economic and social position of the parties to a dispute acts in favour of the powerful, who will be in a better position to exploit strict rules. This is the case, for example, with the creditor who distrains for debt or the landlord who evicts for non-payment of rent, where superior knowledge, connections and capacity to endure lengthy litigation will be telling factors, and even more so where the law allows powers of self-help.

Secondly, every legal system creates hierarchies in which certain individuals have the power to make decisions as to the fate of others. Such authority, and in particular the direction that its exercise may involve, can be used by its holder unfairly, or for purposes other than that for which it is intended.

An abuse of either type is difficult to impugn because it usually remains within the letter of the law or at most bends the rules without breaking them even while constituting the most flagrant injustice. Paradoxically, an outright breach of the law, such as bribery or intimidation by a litigant or corruption in a judge or administrator, is easier for the legal system to deal with, at least theoretically. In practice, however, if the legal system itself is not functioning effectively, the injured party may still be denied a remedy simply because the wrongdoer has the power to block access to an impartial tribunal or to stultify its actions.

The legal systems of today's industrial democracies are relatively effective in the application of legal norms, so that outright corruption is seldom a problem. Where abuse of power is

---

[1] 16,19.

within, or on the edge of, the law, their record is more mixed. Abuse of authority has been met with various doctrines designed to force the holder of a discretion to exercise that discretion properly.[2] At the same time, the need for finality in administration acts as a restraint on the over-zealous control of discretion, leading to the admission that the authority to decide must sometimes mean the authority to make a bad decision.

Modern systems have been least successful in dealing with abuse of economic power. Equitable doctrines are used sparingly, for fear of upsetting the certainty on which the law depends,[3] and attempts

---

[2]The most famous example is the French doctrine of *détournement de pouvoir*. This is defined as the case where "...une autorité administrative accomplit un acte de sa compétence mais en vue d'un but autre que celui pour lequel l'acte pourait légalement être accompli." (A. de Laubadère, *Traité de Droit Administratif* (8th ed.), Paris 1980, para. 946). The same author lists among the main examples of wrong purpose : "le mobile personnel (intéret privé, esprit de vengeance, de brimade); L'intéret d'un tiers (décision destinée à favoriser un particulier au détriment d'un autre)." (ibid, para 950). Likewise in German law: "Das Ermessen ist pflichtgebunden....Die Pflichtgebundenheit..bedeutet, dass die Verwaltung weder nach Belieben noch nach Willkür verfahren dürfe. Belieben bedeutet ein Handeln, das ausschliesslich subjektiven Erwägungen ohne Zusammenhang mit sachlichen Zwecken entspringt, während als Willkür ein Handeln aus sachfremden Motiven zu bezeichnen ist." (E. Forsthoff, *Lehrbuch des Verwaltungsrechts*, Vol. I, München 1973, p.97).

In fact, the doctrine is no different in Common Law jurisdictions, although it has developed under the narrow guise of interpretation of the statute giving a discretionary power to see if the exercise of that power was within the terms of the statute. But this means not only the express words of the statute but also those terms implied by the court. Thus in *Rooke's* case, the Commissioners of Sewers had levied charges for repairing a river bank, but they had thrown the whole charge on one adjacent owner instead of apportioning it among all the owners benefited. In law they had power to levy charges in their discretion. Nonetheless this charge was disallowed as inequitable, for: "....notwithstanding the words of the commission give authority to the commissioners to do according to their discretions, yet their proceedings ought to be limited and bound with the rule of reason and law. For discretion is a science or understanding to discern between falsity and truth, between wrong and right, between shadows and substance, between equity and colourable glosses and pretences, and not to do according to their wills and private affections..." ((1598) 5 Co. Rep. 99b). This doctrine, established in the sixteenth century, is still the basis of the modern law. (See H.W.R. Wade, *Administrative Law* 5th edition, Oxford 1982, 351-360).

[3] A notable exception is the case of *Sir Lindsay Parkinson & Co. Ltd. v. Triplan Ltd* [1973] Q.B. 609. The plaintiffs, Triplan, were a small company acting as sub-contractors to the defendants, a large public company. Triplan sued the defendants for outstanding balances on their sub-contracting work but the latter, hearing that Triplan were in financial difficulties, applied for an order for security for costs before the matter could come to trial. The court may order that the plaintiff give security for the defendant's costs of the action if *inter alia* there is reason to believe that the plaintiff will be unable to pay the costs of the defendant if his action fails. On the face of it the defendants had an unassailable case, but in fact their delaying tactics were in part responsible for the plaintiffs' want of means and the effect of the order would

(continued on next page)

to establish protected categories of persons or transactions frequently have the opposite effect to that intended, creating traps for the unwary, a refuge for scoundrels, and even leading to the complete disappearance of the economic activity that they were supposed to regulate.[4]

How did the systems of the Ancient Near East fare when faced with such problems? Their task was considerably more difficult. On the one hand, lacking the material resources of a modern industrial state, they could not hope to be so effective in applying the rule of law; corruption and intimidation were bound to be a problem. On the other hand, the separation of powers was less developed - not only administrative and judicial authority might be found in the same hands but economic and social power as well.[5] Furthermore, self-help was more prevalent as an acceptable means of realizing legal rights. There was therefore considerable scope for abuse of power within the letter of the law as much as outside it.

B. MESOPOTAMIA

The Mesopotamian sources leave no doubt as to who is the guardian against abuse of power, whether derived from economic strength or legal authority. The king acts both as the fountainhead of law in the strict sense and as the guarantor of social justice.[6]

A common literary topos informs us of what the king considers to be his duty in this field. King Urukagina[7] of Lagash declares that he would not deliver up the widow and orphan to the powerful,[8] a

---

have been to stifle a genuine claim before it could be heard. The court held that in such circumstances it had a discretion not to order security for costs from the plaintiff. Counsel for Triplan, Mr. Gerald Levy, unconsciously tapped a very ancient stream of authority (see below) when he argued (p.622): "an order for security must not be the means of preventing a plaintiff who has a reasonably arguable cause of action from coming to the judgment seat or be a weapon of oppression for the strong against the weak."

[4] A good example is tenant protection legislation, which makes it extremely difficult to find accommodation of the protected category.

[5] For example, the "elders", who were the heads of leading local families. See *Theologisches Wörterbuch zum Alten Testament* (TWAT) Vol. II Cols. 644-650.

[6] The king upholds *kittum*, which is justice achieved by ensuring that the correct procedures are followed (see CAD Vol. K, 470 sub *kittu* A 1(b)) and *mīšarum*, which is justice achieved by correcting distortions in the economic or legal system (see CAD Vol. M Pt 2, 117 *sub mīšaru* 1 and 2(a). M. Weinfeld has shown that when the two terms are used together, they form a hendyadis meaning "social justice": *Justice and Righteousness in Israel and the Nations*, Jerusalem 1985 12-18. (in Hebrew).

[7] The Sumerian Dictionary reads this name Uruinimgina. See Volume B, Bibliographical abbreviations, p. xxv.

[8] nu-síg nu-ma-su lú-á-tuku nu-na-gá-gá-a: M. Lambert, "Les 'reformes' d'Urukagina" *RA* 50(1956) 182-183. Lambert translates lú-á-tuku "riche", but this would be more suitable for lú- níg-tuku. See next note.

theme expanded upon by King Ur-Nammu of Ur in his boast: "The orphan I did not deliver up to the rich man; the widow I did not deliver up to the mighty man; the man of one shekel I did not deliver up to the man of one mina; the man with one sheep I did not deliver up to the man with one ox."[9] Likewise King Hammurabi of Babylon considers it his task "that the strong might not oppress the weak, that justice be given to the orphan and widow."[10]

The orphan and widow might not necessarily be poor, but they shared with the poor an extreme vulnerability to the abuses that we have described above. The remedy therefore lay not merely in the proper enforcement of the letter of the law but in administrative reforms and extra-judicial measures.

Urukagina issued a reform whereby the privileges of certain offices that had given rise to exploitation were revoked.[11] Various Babylonian kings issued mīšarum-edicts, whereby debts entered into under perfectly valid contracts were cancelled.[12] But these are drastic steps of such general application that they sweep away the just along with the unjust, without regard to the individual case.

A finer approach is demonstrated by certain paragraphs of the law-codes. CH 34 reads:

> If a captain or a lieutenant takes items of property from a soldier, deprives a soldier of rights, hires a soldier out, delivers up a soldier to a powerful man in a law-suit (or) takes a gift which the king has given to the soldier, that captain or lieutenant shall be put to death.

The list of offences combines acts that would be illegal in any circumstances with others that abuse or take advantage of authority or fail to exercise that authority in the subordinate's favour. The common factor is that the superior expects to succeed in his action because of the authority that is vested in him. It is noteworthy that the duty to protect the subordinate in litigation against the powerful is imposed upon the lower ranks of the administration as well as upon the king.

CH 113 reads:

> If a man is owed corn or silver by a man and without the consent of the owner of the corn he takes corn from the granary or the threshing-floor, once it is proved that he took the corn from the granary or threshing-floor without (the consent of) the

---

[9] See F. Yildiz, "A Tablet of Codex Ur-Nammu from Sippar" *Or.* 50(1981) 87-97, Tablet B lines 30-39, pp. 88, 89, 94-95. nu-síg lú-níg-[tuku]-ra / ba-ra-an-gar/nu-mu-s[u] lú-á-tuku-ra / ba- ra-na-an-gar/ lú- 1 gín-e / lú-1-[m]a-na-ra / ba-ra-n[a]-an-gar /lú-1-udu-ra/ lú-1-gu$_4$ -e / ba-ra-na-an-gar.

[10] Col. XXIV 59-62 (Epilogue). Similarly in the Prologue, col. I 32- 39.

[11] See Lambert (n. 8 above) p. 177, paragraphs 1-5.

[12] Now edited and discussed by F.R. Kraus, *Königliche Verfügungen in Altbabylonischer Zeit*, SDIOAP XI, Leiden 1984.

owner of the corn, that man shall refund as much corn as he took and shall forfeit whatever he lent.

Here is an attempt to counter abuse of economic power. As Driver and Miles point out, the man is not accused of theft, since the verb employed is 'take' (leqû).[13] Moreover, as a creditor, he surely has a right to the corn. His offence must therefore be in abusing that right. The exact nature of the abuse is not clear, but it would seem to lie in excessive self-help. If the creditor rather than the debtor has control over the process of repayment, then he is obviously in a position to take more than is his due. He could presumably distrain a member of the debtor's household in order to force repayment,[14] but he cannot take the bread from the debtor's mouth by using the process of distraint in *substitution* for repayment.[15]

These "laws" derived ultimately from decisions in special cases,[16] which brings us to the main concern of this chapter: the intervention of the king in individual cases of abuse of power. The voluminous correspondence of the Old Babylonian kings shows that the king did concern himself with the most minute details of daily administration, and was constantly intervening in the cases of individuals that had been brought to his attention. There are some indications that individuals injured by abuse of power could bring their case before the king. The procedure involved seems to have been a petition appealing for justice rather than formal appeal from the decision of a lower tribunal. In the most celebrated case,[17] a tribunal confirmed that the petitioner's contract of purchase was not cancelled by a *mišarum* decree and sent his deeds on to a higher official, the "Captain of Barbers". The latter, however, smashed the tablets of deed without hearing the petitioner. The text continues[18]: ".... I collected the pieces of my tablets from his house and showed them to A,B and C (the members of the lower tribunal), but they said: "What can we say to the "Captain of Barbers"?"

"To you, O Divine one, I have come. Let my lord judge for me the case of the breaking of tablets in the absence of judges and of the party himself. Just as the weak would not be delivered to the strong

---

[13] *The Babylonian Laws*, Oxford 1952, Pt. I, p. 214.

[14] Cf. the following paragraphs, 114-116.

[15] The concern to ensure that repayment of a loan remain in the debtor's control seems also to underlie paragraph 49. A creditor's right is a right *in personam*; to allow him a right *in rem* in fungibles plus the opportunity of self-help would leave the debtor in an impossibly weak position in disputes over completion of repayment.

[16] See R. Westbrook, "Biblical and Cuneiform Law Codes" RB 92 (1985) 247-264, esp. 258-264.

[17] Edited by J.J. Finkelstein, "Some New *Misharum* Material and its Implications" *Assyriological Studies* 16 (Studies in Honor of B. Landsberger) 233-251. Finkelstein's interpretation is followed here, with only some minor changes in the translation.

[18] Lines 40-53.

before my lord, let all Sippar see that ... the strong to injure the weak." Before us is a classic case of abuse of administrative power. The official involved was entitled to override the lower tribunal and take the decision that he did, but in doing so he failed, according to the petitioner, to have regard for the principles of procedural justice.[19] The only recourse is a petition to the king, couched in exactly the same terms as the literary topos above, which thus acquires a practical context.

In AbB 1 34, a *naditum* priestess complains to the king (or a high official - the appellation is "my lord") that X had refused to pay her the whole of the price for a garment she had sold him, and when she approached him about the balance, he beat her. He also boasted that he had similarly beaten five other priestesses rather than pay. The priestess appeals in much the same language as in the previous case: "My lord, you are the judge, judge my case with X!"

Why did the priestess not simply take X to a regular court? The reason would seem to be that X is too powerful to be subject to a local tribunal, as his boast indicates. The only, or the best, course open to the priestess is to petition the king, and the same is threatened by the head of a cloister in complaining to an official who has taken the slave of a priestess for military service: "The priestess should not approach *(maharu)* the king!"

Other documents give an account from the king's point of view. In AbB II 6 Hammurabi orders a high official to investigate a miller's complaint that the local mayor took his crop. If the complaint is justified, damages are to be paid and a punishment (unspecified - presumably at the official's discretion) imposed on the mayor. Finally, in AbB II 74, Abi-eshuh orders the judges of Sippar to transfer all the parties and witnesses in a case to Babylon for the hearing, following a complaint that the Sippar court had refused to "do justice" *(šutešuru)* in spite of two years of repeated applications. Apparently the injured parties (in a family dispute) could not appeal from a decision because the court itself had repeatedly refused to hear the case. They therefore petitioned the king directly.

---

[19] Procedural safeguards on administrative acts are in the Common Law subsumed under the heading "natural justice". This is a technical term which comprises two fundamental rules of fair procedure: that a man may not be a judge in his own cause; and that a man's defence must always be fairly heard. The term goes back to medieval precedents, where these rules were considered so obvious as to be part of the natural order of things, as perhaps they are. See Wade (op. cit. n.2 above) Caps. 13 and 15. The case before us falls, of course, under the second rule: the right to a fair hearing.

C. ISRAEL

The duty of the king to protect the rights of the widow, orphan and the poor is not confined to Mesopotamia. As F.C. Fensham has shown, it is a common literary topos throughout the Ancient Near East.[20] In the Bible it is most often applied to God as the divine king.[21] Likewise, the issuing of *mīšarum*-decrees is attested in the Bible as a recognized activity of kings, whether human or divine.[22]

The general picture must therefore have been the same,[23] but our concern is to find evidence of individual instances of abuse of power, and for this purpose we must turn to consider a seemingly unrelated question - the much-disputed terminology of theft and robbery.

D. THE BIBLICAL TERMINOLOGY FOR THEFT AND ROBBERY

There are two principal terms used in the Bible to denote misappropriation of property: *gnb* and *gzl*.[24] From the examples given in the Tannaitic sources,[25] the traditional rabbinic distinction would appear to be that *gnb* refers to theft and *gzl* to robbery, the difference being that theft is committed by stealth; robbery, by open force.[26]

The most serious objection to attributing this distinction to the biblical law is the key passage, Leviticus 5,21-26:

> If anyone sins and commits a breach of faith against the Lord by deceiving his neighbour in a matter of deposit or security, or through robbery *(gzl)* or if he has oppressed (*'šq)* his neighbour or has found what was lost and lied about it, swearing falsely - in any of all the things which men do and sin therein, when one has sinned and become guilty, he shall restore what he took by robbery, or what he got by oppression, or the deposit which was committed to him, or the lost thing which he found, or anything about which he has sworn falsely; he shall restore it in full, and shall add a fifth to it, and give it to him to whom it belongs, on the day of his guilt offering. And he shall bring to the priest his guilt offering to the Lord, a ram without blemish out of the flock, valued by you at the price for a guilt offering; and the priest shall make atonement for him before the Lord, and he shall be forgiven for any of the things which one may do and thereby become guilty. (RSV).

The text reveals three problems. First, this is the only biblical source in which the punishment for robbery is mentioned, and it is remarkably lenient, being less severe than the punishment for

---

[20] "Widow, Orphan, and the Poor in Ancient Near Eastern Legal and Wisdom Literature", *JNES* 21 (1962) 129-139.

[21] Fensham, (n.20 above) 166-167.

[22] See most recently Weinfeld (n. 6 above), Chapters 8 and 9.

[23] See K.W. Whitelam, *The Just King* JSOT Suppl 12, Sheffield 1979, 29-37.

[24] For convenience, the root of the verb is used in quotations unless they are from a secondary source or the grammatical form is of some special importance.

[25] In M. Baba Qamma, Chapter 7 gives examples of *gnb* and Chapters 9 and 10 examples of *gzl*.

[26] See Milgrom (n. 39 below) p. 89.

theft.[27] Secondly, robbery appears to be classified as an offence of deceit, without openness or force. Thirdly, the type of misappropriation which is more akin to the other examples listed, theft, is notable for its absence.

Accordingly, A. Büchler drew the conclusion that the tannaitic distinction was not that of the Bible. In respect of this pericope he observed: "Robbery seems to include theft and any other form of a dishonest removal of the neighbour's property, as it is otherwise difficult to understand why in the full list of the various ways of misappropriation theft should have been ignored."[28] Büchler pointed to a number of other passages where the characteristic feature of robbery, the use of force and violence, was absent. In particular, he identified two extended senses of the term:[29] (1) where rulers deprived the weak of their property by perverting justice when acting in their capacity as rulers,[30] (2) where creditors exercised their legal right of distraint, but with great inhumanity.[31] In the second sense *gzl* is to be compared with *'šq*, both being acts of injustice supported by the application of some law and legal claim.

The difficulty with Büchler's analysis is that the term *gzl* becomes impossibly wide. If it embraces any form of dishonest appropriation, one wonders what function is left to *gnb*. Jackson, therefore, while agreeing with Büchler that the tannaitic distinction is not applicable, presents his own analysis with an added historical dimension.[32]

In the early period of biblical history, *gnb* is used of the act of an individual who is a member of the community, whereas *gzl* denotes the act of an outsider, usually in a group.[33] The latter may constitute an organized band of raiders, even a challenge to central authority. No penalty is therefore found in the law codes, since the response must be more by military than judicial means.[34] Thus in

---

[27] The penalties for theft range from twofold (Ex. 22,3) through four-and fivefold (Ex 21,37) to sevenfold (Prov. 6,30-31). Jackson (see n. 32 below) suggests that the penalty in Lev. 5,25 was in fact twofold plus a fifth. This is achieved by assuming the guilt-offering to be equivalent in value to the property misappropriated (p.175). Even if this interpretation is accepted, it still leaves *gzl* low down in the table of penalties, and the victim with less compensation, since he is not the recipient of the guilt-offering.

[28] A. Büchler, *Studies in Sin and Atonement in the Rabbinic Literature of the First Century*, London 1928, p. 375.

[29] *Ibid.* 376-378.

[30] Is. 3,13-15; Mic. 2,2; 3,2-3.

[31] Is. 61,8; Job 24,9.

[32] B. Jackson, *Theft in Early Jewish Law*, Oxford 1972.

[33] *Ibid.* p. 6.

[34] *Ibid.* 180-181. Jackson (13-14) notes a reference in Ex. 22,9-10, where the shepherd is not liable for loss caused by raiders (*šbh=gzl*).

Jud. 9,25 the lords of Shechem resisted Abimelech's rule by ambushing *(gzl)* travellers in the hills.[35] Likewise in Jud. 21,23 the verb *gzl* is used of the Benjaminites who raid their neighbours to capture brides. And most interesting of all is the opposing use of *gnb* and *gzl* in the confrontation between Jacob and Laban in Gen. 31, 27-31. Laban accuses Jacob of stealing *(gnb)* his household goods, while Jacob asserts that Laban was about to rob *(gzl)* him of his wives, Laban's daughters. According to Jackson, the subtlety here is that Laban by using *gnb* asserts that Jacob is an insider, a member of the household, while Jacob by using *gzl* asserts his independence.[36] With the establishment of central authority under David, however, the practical danger from outside raiders diminished, and the distinction between the two terms became blurred. The use of *gzl* changes. It was taken over by the prophets as a polemical term for economic exploitation and as a result lost its association with raiding groups (a gap which was in turn covered by *gnb* as the more general term).[37]

This brings us to the later legal sources, the Holiness Code and the Priestly Code, and thus to the key text, Lev. 5,21-26. In Jackson's view *gzl* here represents *gnb* of the Covenant Code, the passage being an attempt to restate the earlier law. The text, however, is composite and in the final version *gzl* is subsumed, not altogether successfully, under the principle of *khš* whose exact import is uncertain.[38]

Jackson's analysis has been strongly criticized by Milgrom.[39] As far as the early period is concerned, Milgrom points out that there are a number of texts where *gnb* is used for theft by an outsider. Thus in the theft of Joseph's cup in Gen. 44,8, Joseph's brothers are clearly outsiders to Egyptian society.[40] Jackson argues that since it is in the brothers' own speech that the verb is used, it may have been an attempt to tone down their apparent offence.[41] This is not very convincing, since the brothers were obviously not insiders, and equally obviously not armed robbers, so that it is difficult to see what mitigating factor could lie in the theft being committed by an insider.

The term *gnb* is also used to describe the removal of the corpses of Saul and his sons from Beth Shean by the men of Jabesh-Gilead.[42]

[35] *Ibid.* 6-7.

[36] *Ibid.* 7-8.

[37] *Ibid.* 10-11.

[38] *Ibid.* 53-58.

[39] J. Milgrom, *Cult and Conscience*, Studies in Judaism in Late Antiquity XVIII, Leiden 1976.

[40] *Ibid.* p. 91.

[41] *Theft* p. 9.

[42] I S. 31,12; 2 S. 21,12.

Jackson tries to give the offenders insider status as "members of a neighboring community in the period after the establishment of the monarchy."[43] But as Milgrom points out,[44] Beth Shean was at the time still in the hands of the Philistines, and therefore not part of the monarchy. There is nothing to distinguish their act from that of the Benjaminites, except that, not having the strength to confront the Philistines, they were obliged to operate by stealth.

Turning to the later period, Milgrom raises objections to the idea that the two terms became so blurred that they could share the same semantic range. Lev. 19,11.13 prohibits both gnb and gzl in a long list of offences, so that they cannot be synonymous. Nor can it be argued that the use of gzl is polemical, as in the prophetic sense of exploitation, since it lacks a figurative context, being merely part of a list. This is borne out by Lev. 5,21.23, where it is in a legal context, a list of offences with penalties attached, and must therefore be a specific crime. Finally, if as Jackson argues, the latter passage is a restatement of the Covenant Code, there would seem no good reason for substituting gzl for the original gnb.[45]

Milgrom's conclusion is that the tannaitic distinction between gnb as theft, characterized by stealth, and gzl as robbery, characterized by open force, must be correct for biblical law.[46]

Accordingly, he explains the differentiation of terms in the Jacob-Laban confrontation as a simple reflection of the balance (or rather imbalance) of power. As paterfamilias, Laban could move against Jacob forcibly, whereas Jacob, as a client, could only get the better of Laban by stealth.[47]

Since any historical development is denied, Milgrom is obliged to defend the thesis that gzl refers to a forcible act not only in the prophetical use of the term, but also in Lev. 5,21-26. To do so, he

[43] Theft p. 91.

[44] Cult and Conscience p. 91.

[45] Ibid. 92-93.

[46] Ibid. 93. The exact meaning of the term gnb is not relevant to our inquiry, which is concerned only with the term gzl. We would point out, however, that neither Jackson's nor Milgrom's definition takes sufficient account of the vital difference between legal and non-legal contexts. Secrecy is not usually part of the legal definition of theft; the important factor is misappropriation. Violence may aggravate the offence, but whether it is secret or open (as in the case of larceny by a trick) is of little consequence in law. Thus in modern English law, a person is guilty of theft if he "dishonestly appropriates property belonging to another with the intention of permanently depriving the other of it..." (Theft Act 1968 s.1(1)), with not a word about secrecy. It is not surprising, therefore, that in legal texts in the Bible, gnb may cover examples of non-secret theft, such as the kidnapping of persons sui iuris (Jackson, p. 5). In the popular mind, on the other hand, secrecy is often seen as a characteristic of theft, as in modern English parlance (see the OED entry on 'stealth'). It is not surprising, therefore, that gnb is used in non-legal texts in the Bible as a simile for secrecy (e.g. Prov. 9,17).

[47] Ibid. p. 91.

engages in a complex process of reasoning based on the association of *gzl* with another term found in the Prophets and in Leviticus: '*šq* .[48] It is necessary for us to follow this reasoning in detail:

(1) '*šq* is the product of open force. Evidence is a series of texts where the committers of '*šq* are said to have power,[49] and the cumulative parallelism *lqh*, '*šq*, *rṣṣ* in I S. 12,3-4.

(2) '*šq* has a near synonym in the term *ḥbl* (and '*bṭ*). The latter means to distrain a pledge, which is a forcible act. In Ezekiel, *ḥbl* is associated with '*šq*,[50] and is a crime when the pledge is not restored. Therefore withholding a pledge must be an instance of '*šq*.

(3) Since *ḥbl* and '*bṭ* are aspects of '*šq*, the latter too must be a forcible act.

(4) *gzl* is the product of open force: Dt. 28,29-33.

(5) In the same passages cited by the author in Ezekiel, *gzl* is used in parallelism with *ḥbl*.

(6) Therefore, both *gzl* and '*šq* refer to the illegal withholding of property. The difference between them is that in '*šq* the acquisition is legal whereas in *gzl* it is illegal.

(7) The acquisition is illegal in the case of *gzl* because it refers to the distraint of life-essentials, which is a violation of pentateuchal law and hence equivalent to robbery. It is true that the law only specifies garments and millstones in its prohibitions, but these serve as general categories for all life essentials such as land, farm animals and persons.

Before continuing to Milgrom's analysis of Lev. 5,21-26, we wish to pause and consider the above line of reasoning, since we reject practically every step in it.

(1). Power is not necessarily synonymous with force. It may derive from authority, influence or economic superiority. One must beware of reductionism: an act such as the confiscation of property may have the backing of a sanction to ensure compliance and that sanction may ultimately involve the use of force, but that does not mean that the confiscation itself is a forcible act.[51]

The list in I S. 12, 3-4 concerns legal authority. It is given by Samuel himself as examples of the corrupt practices of a judge and in fact contains more parallels than quoted by Milgrom: "... whose ox have I taken? or whose ass have I taken? or whom have I

[48] *Ibid.* 94-102, esp. p. 99.

[49] Mic. 2,1-2; Job 35,9; Eccl. 4,1.

[50] See *ibid* p. 95 for the parallels.

[51] Milgrom does not define "forcible", but it must be presumed to mean an act of direct physical violence, and not merely one which is contrary to the will of the victim. Otherwise the change of an entry in the land register could be considered forcible.

defrauded (*'šq*)? whom have I oppressed (*ršṣ*)? or from whose hand have I taken ransom-money or a bribe?[52] The taking of bribes is certainly illegal and immoral, but it is not forcible.

(2) and (3). We assume for the sake of argument that Milgrom is right in interppeting *ḥbl* to mean distrain, but it does not follow that it is an aspect of *'šq*.[53] Where in Ezek. 18 non-return of a pledge and *gzl* are listed together, and then *gzl* and *'šq*, there is obviously some connection between the three, but they do not thereby become parallels or overlapping concepts, any more than they would with the other sins listed, such as intercourse with a menstruating woman (v.6). If we accept Milgrom's conclusion that failure to return a pledge is an instance of *'šq*, then *ḥbl* and *'šq* are consecutive actions (the taking of the pledge and its non- return), not synonymous ones.[54]

At all events, the one express example of *'šq* furnished by the Bible rules out force as a necessary component. This is, as Milgrom himself notes, the withholding of a hired worker's wages.[55] By no stretch of the imagination could this be a forcible act; it does not even involve the victim's property, being a failure to fulfil contractual obligations. (4). That *gzl* can involve open force is undisputed. But the fact that it is used in tandem with *'šq* does not necessarily mean that it is the forcible aspect which is the common link. We are not certain that the passage cited from Dt. 28,29-33, in which both verbs occur, refers to enemy action; it seems to us rather that personal enemies are in question in v.31, since one's property is *given* to one's enemies (i.e. by a third party). (5)-(7). There is no law in the Bible forbidding the distraint of life-essentials, nor can such a law be extrapolated from the prohibitions on millstones and garments. To interpret these single instances as symbolic of a much wider category is unhistorical, reflecting post-biblical exegesis rather than biblical reality.[56]

The express prohibition on taking the millstone as pledge is

---

[52] See R. Gordis, "'Na'alam' and Other Observations on the Ain Fashka Scrolls", JNES 9 (1950) 44-47.

[53] As opposed to a pledge given at the time of receipt of the loan. For the arguments on this point, see Milgrom, *ibid.* 95-98.

[54] One should not make too much of the single instance of distraint as such being listed alongside *gzl* (v.16). A good man does not in principle distrain, but should he do so, he must at least return the distress as soon as payment is offered. On pp. 98-9 the verb *ḥbl* is first defined by Milgrom as distraining and then as withholding a pledge. The latter would appear to be an error, in view of the author's interpretation of *ḥbl* in v. 16 (p. 95).

[55] Dt. 24,14-15.

[56] That the prohibition is on a single item is significant. The system in the Ancient Near Eastern law codes whereby wider categories were created was to make lists of items. e.g. "house, wife, slave, slave-girl, ox, ass, or anything of your neighbour's..." (Ex 20,17); "silver, gold, slave, slave-girl, ox, sheep, ass or anything else..." (CH 7).

intended as an exception to the creditor's general right to distrain. The prohibition on garments is not even as wide, applying only to widows,[57] and otherwise being an injunction to return it by the evening,[58] which assumes the right to take it in the first place. To deduce from these two examples a prohibition covering land,[59] animals and persons[60] would leave very little that could be distrained. Reformulating the rule from the positive point of view, i.e. that only luxury items could be distrained, illuminates its unreality.

We now turn to Milgrom's explanation of Lev. 5,21-16. Even if the view that *gzl* is always a forcible act is rejected it does not follow that it must be a species of deceit, and the problem of its inclusion in the list - and the ommission of *gnb* - remains.

Milgrom's first postulate is that the false oath mentioned in this passage applies to all the offences listed.[61] In consequence: "The common denominator of all the cases in Lev 5:20ff. is that the claimant feels certain that he can identify the possessor of his object. However, since he cannot produce witnesses or documents, the possessor needs but to assert his ownership under oath in order to retain the contested object. Thus it should be clear that ordinary theft (*gnbh*) has no place in this series. Theft, by definition, means that the object has been separated from its owner without his knowledge; hence, he has not seen the thief. Since the point of this law is to list only these cases that culminate in the possessor's false oath, it would therefore be pointless to include the term "theft" which assumes that the possessor-thief is unknown."[62]

Milgrom admits that there are cases where the thief is tracked down or the stolen goods identified by their owner, but claims that they are rare. Accordingly they are accounted for in the general clauses on false oath at the end of the protasis (vv.22.24).[63]

The scenario thus produced bears little relation to reality:

1. Milgrom does not state to what purpose witnesses or documents should be produced, but we see no reason why they should not be

---

[57] Dt. 24, 17

[58] Ex. 22,25; Dt. 24,12-13.

[59] It is doubtful whether land can be classified with moveables in this context. *ḥbl* and *'bṭ* are never used in connection with land; only things or persons that can be physically seized.

[60] The prophet Elishah assumes distraint of persons to be legal. He does not aid the prophet's widow in resisting her creditor, but ensures that she obtains the means to pay him and thus free her sons (2 K 4, 1-7).

[61] *Ibid.* p. 85.

[62] *Ibid.* p. 100.

[63] *Ibid.*

available to identify the owner's property. This is exactly the procedure described in CH 9, where the thief is identified by the evidence of the purchase. Nor do we see why the thief should be harder to identify than the finder of lost property, who *is* included in the list.

2. Theft is not by definition without the owner's knowledge. The thief may be identifiable by the owner in the case of larceny by a trick[64] and of misappropriation for example by a borrower, which is admitted by Milgrom to be within the definition of *gnb* in biblical law.[65]

3. Where *gzl* applies to the creditor who refuses to return illegally acquired property, it is not clear why the oath, even if available, should be of decisive significance. An illegally distrained millstone, for example, can be identified and witnesses brought to prove ownership.

4. Finally, the proposed drafting would appear clumsy and unnecessary. If there are cases where the thief is identifiable (and thus called on to take the oath) then there is no reason why theft should not be included in the main list. CH 10 records the case of a thief who fits that category (although, significantly, no exculpatory oath is available to him), so that it cannot have been such a great rarity.

Consequently, we would reject Milgrom's hypothesis also as regards the use of *gzl* in Lev. 5,21-26.

The results so far have not been encouraging. As we have seen, Büchler's definition of *gzl* if far too wide to be acceptable. Jackson's distinction between insider and outsider has been effectively refuted by Milgrom, who shows that it does not fit all the texts, even within the historical framework postulated by Jackson. And Milgrom's own trenchant attempt to defend the tannaitic distinction founders upon its disregard for legal realities.

This does not mean, however, that we must start again from the beginning. Although we disagree with their conclusions (and to some extent with their method), each of these three eminent scholars have in their research furnished insights upon which it is possible to construct a new hypothesis.

---

[64] In modern English law this is called obtaining property by deception and occurs when "A person ... by any deception dishonestly obtains property belonging to another, with the intention of permanently depriving the other of it..." (Theft Act 1968, s.15(1)).

[65] *Ibid.* p. 101.

E. THE DUAL MEANING OF *gzl*

Let us begin with Jackson's theory of the early history of *gzl*. His identification of the term with the activities of armed raiders reflects social reality, not only in the Bible, where there are two clear instances in the book of Judges,[66] but also in the Ancient Near East in general. Jackson rightly refers to Codex Hammurabi, which uses two separate verbs: šarāqu, the normal word for theft, including embezzlement, and *habāu,* which is used for robbery.[67]

From other cuneiform sources, we learn that *habāu* is used frequently by kings who boast of raids into enemy territory. It is used without an object to designate the razzia itself, or for the taking of prisoners and booty. By the same token, the term is used for enemy raids on home territory.[68] It is also applied, however, not to armies but to bands of outlaws who raid herds or kidnap or rob travellers.[69] The picture is very much that already painted by Jackson.

CH treats robbery differently from theft.[70] Paragraphs 22-24 read:

> If a man has committed robbery *(hu-ub-tam ih-bu-ut)* and is caught, that man shall be put to death. If the robber is not caught, the man who has been robbed shall prove whatever he has lost before a god, and the city and the mayor in whose territory or district the robbery has been committed shall replace whatever he has lost. If it is life (i.e. a case of murder), the city and the mayor shall pay one mina of silver to his family.

A number of important points emerge from this law.

1. Robbers are often not caught. The reason is obvious: they come from outside and return to a safe hiding place. As Jackson points out, the most appropriate measures against them are not judicial but military.[71]

2. The helplessness of the courts in this situation is recognized by the imposition of responsibility on the local authority - not to apprehend the criminals but to compensate the victims from the public purse.

---

[66] 9,25; 21,23.

[67] *Theft* p. 11.

[68] See the references in CAD Vol A Pt. I 10-11 *sub haba-tu.*

[69] CAD, *ibid.* E.g. KAR 147 r.12: "he must not go on a trip (or else) robbers will kidnap him (*hab-ba-tu₄ i-hab-ba-tu-šu*); Boissier DA p.10: "he will chance upon a den of robbers but will not be stripped" (nu *ih-ha-bat*). Note that the references in CAD both for this and the previous note are by no means confined to the period of Hammurabi.

[70] For an analysis of the theft paragraphs of CH, see Chapter Four below.

[71] *Theft* 180-181.

3. *habātu* involves violence, even murder, as well as theft.
4. Robbery by armed bands was a problem even under a strong centralized authority such as Hammurabi's kingdom.

This last point is evidence against Jackson's theory of historical development. The existence of robbers is not ended simply by the establishment of a central authority and it is therefore unlikely that David's ascent to the throne led to the disappearance of this particular use of *gzl*. Moreover, it is known that the problem existed in the city-states of Syria in the latter part of the second millenium and was dealt with in the same way as in CH. A series of treaties between Ugarit and its neighbours makes each signatory State or its guild of merchants responsible for compensation when a merchant from the co-signatory State is robbed and murdered in its territory and the perpetrators are not captured.[72]

Indeed, the same solution (and by implication the same problem) can be shown to have still been in application in Israel towards the end of the monarchy. In Dt. 21, 1-9 the victim of an unknown murderer is found in the open fields. The authorities of the nearest town must bring a heifer to a stream and take an exculpatory oath over it. The connection with CH 23-24 has been noted,[73] and the circumstances of the death, the fact that the victim was "pierced (with a sword)"[74] and the responsibility of the local authorities[75] all point to the activities of armed robbers and the difficulty of bringing them to justice.

We must therefore accept that there was no historical development; throughout the biblical period *gzl* was capable of referring to armed robbery. But, as Büchler pointed out, this cannot be the meaning of the verb in most of the contexts in which it appears in the Bible since the perpetrators are established members of society. Nor, as Milgrom has demonstrated, can it be taken in those contexts as a mere rhetorical usage. The verb must therefore have had two different contemporaneous meanings.

---

[72] RS 17.230, 17.146, 18.115, 18.19. Edited by J. Nougayrol in *Le Palais Royal d'Ugarit* IV (=*Mission de Ras Shamra* IX), Paris 1956, 152-160. For a discussion of the implications for biblical law, see R. Westbrook, "Lex Talionis and Exodus 21, 22-25" *RB* 93 (1986) 62- 64.

[73] H. McKeating, "The Development of the Law on Homicide in Ancient Israel" *VT* 25(1975) 46-68 at p. 62 n. 21; A. Phillips, "Another Look at Murder" *JJS* 28(1977) 105-126 at pp. 124-126.

[74] *ḥll*. See Koehler-Baumgartner, 3rd ed. p. 307.

[75] Both the authors cited in n.73 above stress that the exculpatory oath is unique to the biblical law. This is not correct. In a letter from the King of Carchemish to the King of Ugarit concerning a woman whose husband was murdered in the city of Arzigana, an almost identical oath is imposed on the "men of Arzigana" (i.e. the local notables); "we did not kill the husband of the woman, brother of X, in the city. We do not know who killed him." *Ugaritica* V No 27, pp. 95, 97, lines 46-50. See further R. Westbrook, *op. cit.* n. 72 above, 64-65.

If we look at the identity of the perpetrators of *gzl* in cases other than armed robbery, we see that they fall into two groups: members of government (in the broad sense) and the wealthy. In the first group we find the "people of the land",[76] the elders,[77] "those who decree iniquitous decrees"[78] and the heads of Jacob and princes of the house of Israel.[79] The second group is not so closely defined, except in so far as it is identified with one figure: the creditor.[80] Their victims in both cases are the poor, the weak, the widow, orphan and stranger. At first sight, it would seem that nothing could be further from the situation in armed robbery, where the victims would tend to be richer (and certainly more established) than the perpetrators. Paradoxically, however, it is from the status of the parties and the relationship between them that, in our opinion, the analogy with armed robbery may be deduced.

A distinctive feature of armed robbery in the legal sources, which marks it off from theft, is the law's recognition that the victim has little chance of obtaining redress from the robbers through the normal judicial process.[81] Hence the provision for compensation from the public purse. The same applies where a member of the establishment wrongfully takes advantage of his office or economic power in order to take property from the poor and weak. The way to justice is blocked by the very people responsible for providing justice.

In the case of government officials, a striking illustration is provided by Eccl. 5,7: "If you see oppression (*'šq)* of the poor and denial *(gzl)* of law and justice in a province, do not be shocked at the sight: for each high official is being watched by his superior, and they by theirs."[82] It is a succinct description of a corrupt administration. Facing the poor is a veritable "hierarchy of exploiters"[83] who are safe in their actions because each is an offical and recourse is only to other equally corrupt officials.

The sources also provide practical examples of *gzl* by the rich.

---

[76] Ezek. 22,29. The term refers to a governing body. See THAT II 229-230.

[77] Is. 3,14.

[78] Is. 10,1-2. But note that the JPS translation appears to interpret these as private legal documents drafted by the wealthy: "Those who write out evil writs and compose iniquitous documents."

[79] Mic. 3,1-2.

[80] Ezek. 18,8.12.16.17; 33,15; Job 24,2.9. Unspecified: Ps. 35,10; Prov. 22,22; Job 20,19.

[81] It should be remembered that in Ancient Near Eastern Law it is the victim who brings an action for theft, not the public authority. See Chapter Four below.

[82] Translation of these somewhat laconic lines differs greatly, but most scholars interpret the passage as describing administrative corruption. See e.g. R.B.Y. Scott, *Proverbs/Ecclesiastes*, Anchor Bible, New York 1965, 228, and H. Prévost, "L'oppression dans la Bible", Mélanges Prévost, Paris 1982, 3-16, 7.

[83] R.B.Y. Scott, *loc. cit.* (n. 82 above).

Firstly, they abuse the legal right of distraint, not by failing to return pledges[84] but apparently by taking them from persons who will be unable to redeem them,[85] perhaps because the pledge represents their only source of income.[86] A further possibility is that the particular distraint was not legally justified, an offence which gives rise to penalties in the Ancient Near Eastern law codes and which will be discussed in the following chapters. The mention of removing landmarks and taking (gzl) flocks in Job 24,2 may be an indication of this, as may be the payment of compensation (voluntarily!) therefor in Ezek. 33,15.

Secondly, the rich abuse the legal process itself. Prov. 22,22 states: "Do not rob (gzl) the weak because he is weak, or crush the poor at the gate." The "gate" is of course a reference to the law-court, and the "robbery" therefore takes place in the legal proceedings.[87] The rich litigant takes advantage of his poor opponent's inability to present his case, for the text continues: "For the Lord will plead their cause, and will rob those who rob them of life." (v.23).

The overall picture, then, is the same as that which we have seen in the cuneiform sources earlier in the chapter. There are two types of abuse - of administrative power and of economic power.[88] As we noted in the earlier context, there was no separation of administrative and judicial powers, and the holders of such powers will inevitably be members of the wealthy classes.[89]

Abuse of authority, we suggest, provides a satisfactory explanation of the much-disputed use of terms in the quarrel between Jacob and Laban. Jacob expresses his fear that Laban would rob (gzl) him of his daughters.[90] Note that Jacob does not say "my wives". The implication is that Jacob recognizes that Laban might have a certain claim to take back Rachel and Leah in spite of their being married,[91] perhaps if Jacob were guilty of some wrongdoing.

---

[84] In Ezek. 18, 7 and 33,15 gzl and failing to return a pledge are listed separately. Note especially in 33,15 that a person returns a pledge but pays (šlm) compensation for gzl.

[85] Job 24,8.

[86] Job 24,2-3.

[87] Possibly also in Ezek. 22,19.

[88] Ps. 28,24 seems to fit neither use of gzl: "He who robs (gzl) his father and his mother and says he has done nothing wrong - he is next thing to a parricide." It is difficult to see what specific act is involved here. We tentatively suggest that the background is impotent old age, when the parents are dependent on their son for support. If he exploits their helplessness to deprive them of their property while they are still alive (i.e. anticipates his inheritance), it is as if he had already put them in the grave.

[89] See n. 5 above.

[90] Gen. 31,31.

[91] Cf. Gen 30,25-26 and the remarks of Büchler (op. cit. n. 28 above) 377 n. I.

But who is to judge the case? The *paterfamilias* is Laban. He is the ultimate authority, but in this instance he is also a judge in his own cause.[92] Thus Jacob accuses him of (potential) abuse of his authority.

For Jacob there was no remedy but to escape from Laban's jurisdiction. For most victims, however, this would not be a feasible course of action. The question therefore arises whether the Bible offers an alternative remedy. In fact it offers two.

The first possibility has been mentioned in passing above. In Ezek. 33,14-15 a wicked man, who has been guilty of a number of sins, including failure to restore pledges and *gzl*, is threatened with death by God and repents. Accordingly, he voluntarily restores the pledges and pays compensation for his *gzl*. Thanks to an insight of Milgrom, we now know that the same process is being described in Lev. 5,21-26.

The meaning of '*šm* in the Priestly legislation has long defied the efforts of scholars. In the matter that concerns us,[93] its function as a verb in v.23 is obscure. The RSV rendering cited above "...when one has sinned and become guilty" is, as Jackson points out, little short of a tautology.[94] The solution is provided by Milgrom:[95] " ... '*šm* without an object does not refer to a *state* of guilt, but...denotes the suffering brought on by guilt expressed now by words such as remorse and contrition. '*šm* would then mean to be conscience-smitten...." The verse should therefore be translated: "When one thus sins and then feels guilt".

Such feelings do not arise *ex nihilo*. A person has suffered some calamity, such as an illness, which he would naturally consider to be punishment for some sin. His efforts are therefore directed towards the discovery of the specific offence which gave rise to his plight. He can then hope to allay further divine punishment, and cure his disease, by making appropriate reparation.[96] This is the case in the Akkadian *šurpu* ritual, where the incantation priest asks the gods to absolve the curse against the patient, who is ill and distraught through committing some sin. In our opinion, our text derives from the same ancient priestly tradition.[97]

In our text the sufferer has committed an offence for which he would not normally be called to account in an earthly court. His

---

[92] This is a breach of the first head of 'natural justice'. See n. 19 above and Wade (*op. cit.* n. 2 above) Cap. 14.

[93] For a discussion of the question of '*šm* as a whole, see Milgrom , *Cult and Conscience* Chapter I.

[94] *Theft* p. 176.

[95] *Cult and Conscience* 8-9.

[96] *Ibid.* p. 8.

[97] See the seminal article of M.J. Geller, "The Šurpu Incantations and Lev. V. 1-5" JSS 25(1980) 181-192, p. 182.

suffering, however, has caused him to confess and voluntarily make reparation. Hence the penalty is much lighter than would normally be expected or than is the case for theft; confession must be encouraged and usually results in mitigation.[98] The common factor in all the offences then, is that the victim has no remedy, a situation which can arise either because of the perpetrator's unassailable position or the circumstances or his false oath. In the first category fall offences of abuse of power, namely *gzl*, *'šq* [99] and *tswmt yd* [100] and possibly *pqdwn* (deposit) if the bailee is a warehouse owner who can take advantage of the bailor, for example a poor peasant who needs to store his crop. But since the oath procedure is in certain circumstances available to the bailee,[101] it may be false oath that is implied.

In the case of the finder, we suggest that it is the circumstances that work in his favour in being able to deny that the property claimed belongs to the original owner. He may have been able to take an exculpatory oath, but that would only help him if there were no extraneous evidence.

The absence of the thief from the list can be explained on two grounds. Firstly, if, as we have suggested, this text belongs to the same tradition as *šurpu*, then the list was certainly not exhaustive, but only an abstract or summary. The Akkadian text contains a list, recited by the priest, of nearly one hundred offences. They cover the full range of sins mentioned by both biblical priests and prophets: impiety, impurity, infidelity, dishonesty, false oath, violence, oppression, and more. Indeed, comparison with the list of offences in Ezek. 18 reveals that this too must have been derived from the

---

[98] As noted by Milgrom, *Cult and Conscience* 117-119.

[99] For the exact meaning of '*šq* see below, Part H.

[100] This term is usually translated "partnership", following the LXX, or "loan, investment" (Rashi, *ad loc.*; see Milgrom *Cult and Conscience* n. 312). We would propose an entirely different interpretation based on the literal meaning "placing of the hand". This is also the literal translation of the term *manus iniectio*. In early Roman law, *manus iniectio* was the procedure whereby a creditor could seize a defaulting debtor and take him away to his private prison. There, although technically still a free man, he could be bound "with cord or fetters of fifteen pounds weight, not less". Ultimately, if he still could not pay, the debtor could be sold as a slave abroad. See H.F. Jolowicz, *Historical Introduction to the Study of Roman Law*, Cambidge 1952, 190-192. Such a procedure is clearly open to abuse and is therefore appropriate alongside *gzl* and '*šq* in our interpretation. Note further that failing to release a man from his bonds, or tightening his bonds, are among the sins listed in *šurpu* (II 29-31). The matter will be discussed in more detail in a projected study of the connections between Ancient Near Eastern and early Roman Law.

[101] Ex. 22,27.

same tradition.[102] The Akkadian source does not mention theft as such, so that it may simply not have been part of this traditional list. On the other hand it does include oppression[103] and a number of false oaths, concerning *inter alia* concealment of property, theft and murder (II 84-6). In our text therefore, the choice of offences may have been more a question of emphasis than of an exclusive legal category.

Secondly, the offenders alluded to in our text all seem to be pillars of the community, who can rely on their standing and credibility to ward off any legal challenge. Thieves, bandits and the like, once in the hands of the court, have far less chance of cheating justice.

The second remedy is that which we would expect from our earlier discussion of the cuneiform sources. There we saw that the king traditionally has the role of protector of the weak against the mighty and is expected to intervene to correct abuse of power. The prophet Jeremiah expects the same of the kings of Judah:

> And to the house of the king of Judah say, "Hear the word of the Lord, O house of David! Thus says the Lord: 'Execute justice in the morning, and deliver from the hand of the oppressor (*'wšq*) him who has been robbed (*gzwl*)....'"[104]

But kings of flesh and blood cannot always be relied upon, and if they fail, it is the divine king who must intervene. We have already seen in Prov. 22,22-23 that it is God who will take up the cause of the poor man denied justice in court. The same hope is expressed by Ps. 35,10: "Who is like you, O Lord, Who saves the poor from one stronger than him, the poor and wretched from his oppressor (*gzlw*)?" Likewise, Isaiah warns: "The Lord will bring a case against the elders of his people and their princes; you have devoured the vineyard, the spoil (*gzlt*) of the poor is in your

---

[102] Ezek. 18 contains eleven separately identifiable offences apart from *gzl*. A table of comparison reveals the following:

Ezek. 18	Tablet II
1. eat on the mountains	1. eat taboo (5)
2. look to idols	2. scorned god (33)
3. adultery	3. adultery (48)
4. menstruant	4. contact with unclean person(98-103)
5. oppress poor	5. oppress weak (18)
6. not return pledge	6. took (wore) neighbour's clothes(i.e. pledged)(50)
7. not feed hungry	7. -
8. not clothe naked	8. not clothe naked (51)
9. usury	9. -
10. shed blood	10. shed blood (49)
11. injustice in court	11. corrupt judgment (III 24)

For the edition of Šurpu, see E. Reiner, *AfO* Beiheft 11, Graz 1958.

[103] II 61 "he oppresses, takes away, causes to be taken away" (*i-hab-bi-lu i-tab-ba-lu ú-šat-ba-lu*).

[104] 21,11-12. Cf. 22,1-3, where the widow, orphan and stranger are also mentioned.

houses" (3,14). The actions of the divine king are described in the same terms as those expected of his human counterpart.

The next matter to consider, therefore, is the procedure whereby royal intervention is secured on behalf of the victim of abuse of power.

F. A PLEA OF *gzl*

When Abraham is residing in the kingdom of Abimelech, he takes advantage of a visit by the king to complain to him concerning a well "that the servants of Abimelech had robbed" (*gzl*). Clearly, these were royal officials, not armed robbers, but neither should we presume that they simply committed an act of violence.[105] Abraham was a client in a foreign kingdom and unable to resist expropriation even if he had a good claim to the well. His recourse is to claim the protection of the king.[106]

Most victims of abuse of power would not be in the fortunate position of having the king come to visit them; they would have to approach him themselves. We have seen from the correspondence of the Old Babylonian kings that persons would petition the king. The Bible contains a very striking example of such a petition, one which gives us a detailed picture of the machinery of this procedure. It is the parable of the poor man's ewe lamb.

G. THE POOR MAN'S EWE LAMB (2 S. 12,1-14)

Nathan presents to David the case of a poor man who had but a single lamb. When a traveller came to a rich man in the same village the latter "was unwilling to take one of his own flock or herd" for the traveller, but took the poor man's lamb instead.

David is outraged and declares "the man who has done this deserves to die; and he shall restore the lamb fourfold,[107] because he did this thing, and because he had no pity". Nathan then reveals that the case is nothing but a parable of David himself. In spite of having ample means and many wives, "You have smitten Uriah the Hittite with the sword, and have taken his wife to be your wife..." David's penalty is to have his own wives taken by others and death (commuted to the death of his child).

The parable is so problematic that its authenticity, in whole or part, has frequently been questioned.[108] Three main difficulties arise:

---

[105] Gen. 21, 25. Note that the well is the object of the verb *gzl*, not Abraham.

[106] In a similar case involving Isaac, the term *'šq* is used (Gen. 26,20): see below.

[107] Sevenfold, according to the LXX.

[108] See U. Simon, "The Poor Man's Ewe-Lamb" *Biblica* 48 (1967) 207-242 at p. 207 n.2 for references to the earlier literature.

(1) What was the offence of the rich man in the parable? The most obvious answer is theft, but if so why is the case brought before the king, rather than the local court?

(2) If it is theft, why are two penalties given, death and multiple restitution?

(3) The parable does not appear to match David's conduct. It concerns only the taking of another man's property, whereas David also committed adultery and murder.[109]

Simon explains the lack of symmetry between the parable and the factual case as a literary device designed to conceal the true analogy of the parable from the listener until he had pronounced sentence unwittingly on himself.[110] But as Jackson points out, this would enable the offender to argue that his case is different and he is therefore not condemned by his own words. Furthermore, it is not the function of the parable to trap the offender by a clever trick, but rather to induce him to self-condemnation by inviting him to judge an analogous case where his judgment is not clouded by personal considerations.[111]

Jackson's own explanation is that the analogy was originally to theft only. David's offence was that of wife-stealing, the stealing of a person not *sui iuris*. Consequently the death penalty in the fable is secondary, since multiple restitution is the proper penalty for theft of a lamb. The reason why the parable did not allude to Uriah's murder is that at the time there was no legal liability for death by indirect causation. Uriah had been killed "with the sword of the Ammonites" (v.9).[112]

There are a number of objections to this theory. Firstly, Seebass points out that if ordinary theft were involved, the case would have been settled before the local court; there is no reason for it to be brought before the king.[113] Secondly, the causal connection between David and the death of Uriah is stated categorically by Nathan, and the text has to be heavily emended in order to excise these references. There are no independent formal grounds for rejecting Nathan's statements as late additions;[114] to say that one

---

[109] See D. Daube "Nathan's Parable" *NT* 24 (1982) 275-288 at pp. 275- 227. Daube reconstructs an original Canaanite fable on the assumption that the present fable does not match the circumstances.

[110] *Op. cit.* (n. 108 above) 223-226.

[111] *Theft* p. 146.

[112] *Ibid.* 146-147.

[113] H. Seebass, "Nathan und David in II Sam 12", *ZAW* 86 (1974) 203-211 at p. 205.

[114] Jackson (*Theft* p.147 n.6) refers to Kittel's suggestion that the last clause of v. 9 is an addition, but it is this clause that Jackson relies upon to show the indirect nature of the killing, and its excision leaves the far more direct statement in the same verse: "You struck down Uriah the Hittite with the sword".

should do so because they have no equivalent in the parable[115] begs the question of what the rich man's real offence was.

A different approach is that of Phillips, who proffers a rationale for the retention of both penalties in David's response in vv. 5-6.[116] Phillips also assumes that the parable is exclusively concerned with theft, but when David uses the term *bn mwt* of the rich man (lit.: 'son of death') he is not referring to a death penalty; on the contrary, it is merely an emphatic expression of the opinion that the man deserves death, while noting regretfully that he can only be sued for multiple damages. According to Phillips, all crimes carry the death penalty but theft is only a tort and the state cannot intervene.[117] The climax then comes with Nathan's disclosure that David is the rich man of the parable. But he is not simply a *bn mwt*, a man who deserves to die, but who can only be sued in tort: he is, by his murder of Uriah, an actual murderer who should suffer execution under Israel's criminal law.[118]

Leaving aside the question of whether the modern distinction between crime and tort can in fact be applied to biblical law,[119] there remains a fundamental objection to Phillips' interpretation: if David's true offence is murder and the penalty is death, why should Nathan have recourse to the parable at all? David deserves to die because he committed an offence carrying the death penalty, and there is an end to the matter. It adds very little to say that he is also a thief and a thief in such aggravated circumstances deserves the death penalty, but will not suffer it.

A further point, which applies not only to Phillips' interpretation, is that the death penalty would appear to be somewhat harsh in the circumstances of the fable, given that the normal penalty is four-fold restitution. The only aggravating circumstances are that the thief was rich (for which the appropriate penalty would be a higher payment)[120] and that the poor man had a sentimental attachment to his property.

We are therefore returned to the primary question: what was the rich man's offence? The correct answer, in our opinion, is given by Seebass: it was not theft but abuse of power, and herein lies the parallel with David's conduct. According to Seebass, the rich man could simply take the poor man's property openly because he had

---

115 Jackson, *ibid.*

116 A. Phillips, "The Interpretation of 2 Samuel xii 5-6", *VT* 16(1966) 242-244.

117 *Ibid.* p. 243.

118 *Ibid.* p. 244.

119 This is the thesis of Phillips' major work *Ancient Israel's Criminal Law*, Oxford 1970.

120 As the LXX assumes in substituting a seven-fold payment, doubtless on the basis of Prov. 6,31, which itself assumes that the thief thereby forfeits all his property. On the penalties for theft, see Chapter Four below.

little to fear from a law-suit - even if found guilty, he could pay the penalty with ease. The poor man, on the other hand, could hardly dare risk threatening proceedings against one so powerful. His only recourse was to seek the king's protection through a third party. In the same way, David could take Uriah's wife without fear of the consequences, since Uriah as his subject had no recourse against him, except before a divine tribunal.[121]

Seebass' interpretation of the parable is certainly feasible, especially in the light of the Mesopotamian letter AbB I 34 that we discussed at the beginning of this chapter, where a woman complains about a powerful customer who beat her rather than pay his bill. It seems to us, however, that a slight variation would produce an even closer symmetry between parable and case. Seebass is forced to exclude the killing of Uriah from consideration altogether, since it is still not mirrored in the parable, although it is a major element in Nathan's condemnation. Nor is it clear that David, albeit king, could simply have taken Uriah's wife from him. Kings in the Ancient Near East could not, and did not, openly flout the rules of law and morality, as the machinations needed by Jezebel to obtain Naboth's vineyard illustrate. It is true that there was no legal sanction, but there was a political sanction, in that a king's power ultimately depends on the loyalty of his followers. King David could hardly rely upon the loyalty of his soldiers if he took away their wives.[122]

We would therefore take up a point made by Simon concerning the passing traveller in the parable. Simon compares a Beduin custom whereby a person who has to entertain an unexpected visitor may take a sheep from his neighbour's herd. There are certain rules to this legalized theft, for example that the taker must be poor and must not take the owner's pet animal. Thus in the parable the sudden arrival of a traveller led to the requisitioning of a ewe in accordance with custom but in breach of the rules, since the host was not poor and the ewe was the owner's pet.[123]

We would not suggest that the details of a modern Beduin custom can be directly imposed upon a biblical narrative, but the perception that the rich man acted in pursuance of a duty to a passing guest seems to us to explain the presence of these details in the parable and to point to the true nature of the rich man's offence. For the text nowhere states that the rich man stole the sheep; it

---

[121] Op.cit. (n. 113 above) 205-206.

[122] The point is well illustrated by Saul's difficulties with the priests of Nob in I S. 22. Although he actually justifies his order to kill them (v. 17: they are guilty of treason), his officers still refuse to execute the royal command and Saul, far from punishing them, is forced to turn to a foreign mercenary.

[123] Op. cit. (n. 108 above) 227-229.

infers that he took it by right,[124] and that his offence was to choose
not to take a sheep of his own. We would reconstruct the scenario of
the parable as follows. A traveller came to the village where the
two parties lived and had to be fed by the village in accordance
with the rules of hospitality. Being a man of some importance, he
was the guest of the rich man. The rich man should naturally have
taken a sheep from his own flock. But having in strict law the right
to take a sheep from anyone in the village for this purpose, he took
the poor man's only ewe-lamb. In other words, the rich man had a
discretionary power which he abused for selfish motives.

David's actions now stand in exact parallel. Nathan accuses him
of two things:[125] "You have killed Uriah the Hittite with the
sword, and have taken his wife to be your wife..." Kings have a
perfect right to send their soldiers to death in battle - it is one of
the normal prerogatives of a king and cannot be qualified as
murder. Nor would there normally be any objection to the king
marrying the widow of one of his fallen soldiers - indeed it might
be considered a noble gesture. But where the king has deliberately
sent the soldier to his death in order to marry the widow - that is
an abuse of his authority for a selfish motive.

This interpretation enables us to explain the circumstances
surrounding the parable. The case was brought before the king
because the ordinary court had no power to intervene. The rich man
had acted within his strict rights. The only course was an extra-
judicial petition to the king, interestingly enough, with the aid of a
powerful intermediary. The nature of the petition also explains
why the death penalty applied - the king, we would suggest, had a
discretionary power of sentencing in such cases, and could impose
the death penalty in aggravated cases, as where the damage was
irreversible or the motive particularly reprehensible.[126] We must
therefore follow those commentators who claim that the second
part of v.6, imposing fourfold restitution in addition, is secondary[127]
- added by a later hand which took the rich man's offence to be
theft and gave the appropriate penalty from the Torah. We are
buttressed in this emendation by the fact that it has no parallel in
the actual case - David naturally assumes his penalty to be death -

[124] Cf. the discussion of CH 113 above, where the verb is also "to take" and not "to steal".

[125] N.B. Nathan does not accuse David of adultery, nor does it appear in the parable.

[126] Where divine justice intervenes, the penalty is assumed by Ezekiel to be death (18,13). Cf. Prov. 22,22-24. In Micah, on the other hand, the penalty appears to be loss of property and status (2,2-5). For Mesopotamia, cf. AbB II 6 discussed above, where the property is to be returned and an unspecified penalty (probably pecuniary) imposed.

[127] See Jackson, Theft 147 n.2.

and that, although its cumulation with the death penalty might be legally feasible, from the literary point of view it is a resounding anticlimax.

Such were the consequences of a petition on the grounds of *gzl*.[128]

H. ABUSE OF POWER BY '*šq*

We have seen that *gzl* is often used in the Bible in conjunction with the term '*šq*. Our examination of the concept of abuse of power would not be complete without considering the relationship between the two terms.

From Jeremiah's use of these terms it might be concluded that they were synonyms: "save the robbed (*gzwl*) from the hand of the oppressor ('*wšq*)".[129] But although they are frequently listed together[130] and occasionally even joined as a couplet,[131] it is clear that there is a distinction between them, albeit a fine one. Thus the passage in Lev. 5,21-26 includes both in a list of related but different offences. We shall begin by showing what they have in common and then consider what is the distinguishing factor.

Like *gzl* in the sense of abuse of power, '*šq* is an offence of the rich and powerful. In two texts in which it appears alongside *gzl*, it is performed, like *gzl*, by the "people of the land"[132] and the provincial administration[133] respectively. Hos. 5,11 names the "lords of Judah" as culprits, while Eccl. 4,1 speaks only of those with power and Ps. 73,8 of it emanating from on high. In I S. 12,4, on the other hand, the prophet in his valedictory address directly ascribes '*šq* to the corrupt judge, a theme which is taken up in the most daring manner by Job, who complains to God that He oppresses ('*šq*) him without cause while favouring the wicked.[134]

The victims are also the same as those of *gzl*; the widow, the

---

[128] In our view the *Meṣad Ḥashavyahu* inscription from the time of Josiah is an example of just such a petition. A worker complains to a royal official that a named person took (*lqḥ*) his garment and has not returned it, in spite of the worker having fulfilled his tasks. The named person is not accused of theft; apparently he had some authority over the worker and took the garment in the exercise of his authority. See J. Naveh, "A Hebrew Letter from the Seventh Century B.C." *IEJ* 10 (1960) 129-139, and J. Teixidor, "Bulletin d'Épigraphie Sémitique", *Syria* 50 (1973) 416-417, no. 102, for a summary of the latest research on the inscription.

[129] 21,12; *ibid.* 22,3.

[130] Lev. 19,13; Ezek. 18,18; 22,29; Mic. 2,2; Eccl. 5.7.

[131] Dt. 28,29; Ps. 62,11.

[132] '*m h 'rṣ* Ezek. 22,29. See note 76 above.

[133] Eccl. 5,7.

[134] 10,2-3. Job here pleads his case with God, asking why God has found against him while accepting the arguments of the wicked. In saying: "Does it seem good to you to oppress('*šq*)? (v.3), Job is suggesting that that is what God's judgment in his case amounts to.

orphan and the stranger,[135] the poor and the weak.[136] An additional victim who appears to be special to *'šq* is the hired labourer (*śkyr*).[137] The offence would therefore appear to be abuse of authority or power, and, as expected, the remedy is a petition to the king, human[138] or divine.[139] The reason for recourse to the latter is lack of confidence in the former, as Psalm 146 makes clear, warning men not to put their trust in princes (v.3), but in God (v.5), who does justice for the oppressed (*'šq*).

The difference between the two types of abuse of power is, we suggest the following. *gzl* always involves the taking away of property. This can be seen most clearly in its literal meaning, "to snatch" (something out of someone's grasp)[140] and in its application to armed robbery. The dual sense of to snatch and to abuse a right gives rise to puns on the term. In Job 24,9 "they snatch (*gzl*) the orphan from the breast and distrain upon the poor," implying that the taking of the infant (as a pledge) is an abuse of the right by rich creditors. In Mic. 3,2 the princes of Israel "snatch (*gzl*) their skin from them and their flesh from off their bones", referring to oppression of their subjects.

Practical expression of the operation of *gzl* is found in Jacob's use of the term to describe Laban's taking his wives away from him by force of his patriarchal authority.[141] Similarly, in Ps. 69,5, the author complains "....that which I did not take away (*gzl*) shall I then return?"

In the one explicit example given of *'šq*, on the other hand, there can be no question of taking away someone's property. According to Dt. 24,14- 15: "You shall not oppress (*'šq*) a hired labourer who is poor and needy ... you shall give him his hire on the day he earns it, before the sun goes down..." We have already seen that the hired labourer appears to be the particular victim of *'šq*. He is not being stripped of his property but is being denied what is due to him,[142] and this, we submit, is the essence of *'šq*. It can be seen in the other explicit example given of *'šq*, the use of false scales by a

---

[135] Jer. 7,6; Ezek 22,7.29; Zech. 7,10; Mal. 3,5.

[136] Dt. 24.14, Jer. 22,7; Am. 4,1; Ps. 72,4; Prov. 14,31; 22,16; 28,3. In Eccl. 5,7 the victim is called *rš*, as is the poor man in the parable of the ewe-lamb.

[137] Dt. 24,14, Mal. 3,5. In Lev 19,13 *gzl* is also mentioned, but the provision relating to the labourer's wages would appear to refer back to *'šq*, which is the main subject.

[138] Jer. 21,12; 22,3 (synonymous with *gzl*); Ps. 72,4.

[139] Is. 38,14 (cf. Prov. 22,22); Ps. 103,6; 105,14; 119,135; Job 35,9 (cf. Dt. 24,14), I Chr. 16,21.

[140] 2 S. 23,21.

[141] Gen. 31,31.

[142] The offence is "holding back" wages : Lev. 19,13.

trader.[143] Here again the client is cheated of his due.[144]

The difference between the two types of abuse emerges in passages where the two terms are listed together, but with different objects. Thus in Dt. 28, 31 it is stated" .... your ass shall be taken away *(gzl)* from before your face and shall not be restored to you...." whereas verse 33 continues on the same theme: "A people you do not know will eat the fruit of your soil and all your labours; you shall be oppressed *('šq)* and downtrodden continually." In the first case property is taken, in the second profits or wages due are denied.

In Mic. 2,2, the distinction is more subtle: "They covet fields and take them *(gzl)*; and houses, and take them away;[145] they oppress *('šq)* a man and his house, a man and his inheritance." In the case of *gzl*, "house" is used in the sense of physical premises, and the reference is to expropriation. With *'šq* "house" means family, and as the second part of the clause reveals, the reference is to denial of inheritance-rights that are due to a nuclear family *(byt 'b)*.

Although the difference is meaningful in legal terms,[146] in practice there is ample possibility for overlapping, as in shown by the disputes over wells in the patriarchal narratives. Abraham, as we have seen, complained that Abi-melech's officials had taken away *(gzl)* a well (Gen. 21,25). In Gen. 26, 19-20, Isaac digs a well and finds water, but "the herdsmen of Gerar quarreled with Isaac's herdsmen, saying. "The water is ours". So he called the name of the well Esek *('šq)*, because they tried to cheat him *(ht 'šqw 'mw)*". We see no reason to follow the Masoretic vocalization *('šq)* or to translate 'contend'(RSV) 'strive' (AV) or the like, or to assume that the root is connected to *'sq* 'business'.[147] The Philistines resented Isaac (26,14), and when he discovered water they claimed it as theirs - which was plainly unjust - and thus deprived him of the fruit of his labours. The root *'šq* is therefore most apposite here, even though the exact force of the hitpa"el form is not certain.

On the other hand, we are not given the exact process by which Abraham was deprived of his well. It could have been the same, in which case one might argue that the verb should have been *'šq* - but this is to split hairs. The same rights can be described in two ways:

---

[143] Hos. 12,8.

[144] Cf. Is. 52,4. As the surrounding verses show, the victim was cheated of a price even in the case of self-sale.

[145] Verb *nš'* . Cf. Akkadian *našû* in the property-transfer formula *našû-nadānu* "take and give". See J.C. Greenfield "*Našû-nadānu* and its Congeners," *Essays on the Ancient Near East in Memory of Jacob Joel Finkelstein* (Memoirs of the Connecticut Academy of Arts and Sciences Vol. XIX, 1977) 87-91.

[146] *gzl* sounds in property law, where the analogous claim would be *in rem*, while *'šq* sounds in obligations, where the claim would be in *in personam*.

[147] K-B (3rd ed.) 846.

as ownership of the well (or its water), in which case deprivation is by *gzl*; or as a right to the water in consideration of being the finder, in which case denial of that right is by *'šq*.[148]

I. SUMMARY

In the legal systems of the Ancient Near East, the administration of justice was faced with the problem of cases of abuse of economic or administrative power which the ordinary courts were powerless to prevent. The abuse involved could range from outright corruption to the more subtle - and perhaps more dangerous - form of adherence to the strict letter of the law in the exploitation of rights or authority while perverting its spirit. Biblical law developed two technical terms for such abuses:[149] *gzl*, where property was taken away from the victim (through which aspect the verb *gzl* acquired a dual function, making exploiters the bedfellows of armed robbers), and *'šq*, where the victim was denied his legal due.[150]

In both the biblical and cuneiform sources the remedy was by petition directly to the king. It was considered to be the king's duty *ex officio* to protect the victims of such abuse, for which purpose he had the power to overturn legally established rights. The king also had a discretionary power to punish the offender, even with the death penalty in aggravated cases.

---

[148] Cf. n. 146 above. The latter is the case with modern oil concessions, the oil being owned by the State. See H. Cattan, *The Law of Oil Concessions in the Middle East and North Africa* New York 1967, 19-20.

[149] Other terms, such as *dk'* and *rṣṣ*, do not appear in any legal passage and seem to be used figuratively, but they may have had some technical meaning, as in IS. 12,3-4.

[150] Akkadian contains a rich variety of words for abuse of power, which require independent investigation. The most common term is *habālu*, which appears to cover the range of both *gzl* and *'šq*, but there is also *mašā'u* and *dâṣu*. On the other hand, we have been unable to find a secondary use of "oppress" for the verb *habātu* "to rob". For the moment, reference must be made to the relevant entries in the CAD. We would mention only one point: W.F. Leemans claims that *habā-tu* can apply also to ordinary theft ("Some Aspects of Theft and Robbery in Old-Babylonian Documents", *RdSO* 32 (1957) 661-666). We disagree, partly on the grounds given by Milgrom, p. 93 n. 334. Further grounds must await a separate study.

CHAPTER TWO: REVENGE, RANSOM AND TALIO

1. INTRODUCTION

The provisions of the Ancient Near Eastern Law Codes on liability for death or injury present a curious paradox.

On the one hand, they are an area of the law where evidence for inter-relation between the Codes is at its strongest. That they were all linked to a common schools tradition is apparent from the recurrence of the same standard legal problems:-

1) The case of an unpremeditated blow in a fight leading to non-permanent injury is discussed in three codes: CH 206, HL 10 and Exodus 21,18-19, and in all three the remedy includes payment of medical expenses. In HL and Exodus an additional payment is required to compensate for the victim's period of recuperation, while CH goes on to consider the case where the blow leads to death, imposing a mild penalty, at which point it is joined by CE (Haddad) 47a and possibly HL 174. Thus while none of the provisions contains a full account, by combining them we gain a picture of a schools problem concerning the consequences of an unpremeditated blow in the course of a fight which is summarized by several of the codes. It is to be noted that the intermediate consequence - of permanent injury - is not discussed in this context by any of the relevant provisions. It was perhaps not part of the standard problem.

2) The case of a blow to a pregnant woman causing a miscarriage, which is discussed in CL(Civil) iii 2'-13', CH 209-213, AL 'A' 21,50-52, HL 17 and Ex.21,22-25.[1] Here the different codes bring in individual refinements whether the foetus was the first child, what stage the pregnancy had reached - while certain common features stand out, such as the weight of the penalty and the distinction between the victim's status as wife, daughter, or slave, which will be discussed below. CL,CH and AL (but not Exodus!)[2] go

---

1 The Exodus law, although it deals with a miscarriage, is in fact primarily concerned with a different legal issue to the other provisions mentioned. For a detailed discussion see Westbrook, "Lex Talionis and Exodus 21, 22-25" *RB* 93 (1986) 52-69, and see further below.

2 See note 1 above and see below under 'Price-Fixing'.

on to consider the case where the blow leads to the death of the woman herself. Again, the overall picture is that various facets of a standard problem are being presented, and confirmation that this problem was indeed studied in the scribal schools comes from YBC 2177, a student exercise in Sumerian from the Old Babylonian period, where it is again recorded with further refinements.[3]

3) The case of the goring ox, which is discussed in CE 54-55, CH 250-252, and Ex. 21,28-32 (+ 35-36). The vital link here is the distinction between an ox which gores for the first time and one whose propensity to gore has been noted and a formal warning thereon conveyed to its owner by the local authority. Such a distinction is the artificial creature of a legal system and its recurrence in all three codes cannot be dismissed as coincidence.[4] CE goes on to discuss the analogous cases of a dangerous dog and a tumbledown wall on the basis of the same distinctions.

4) Where the first two examples occur, they are associated by context with a discussion of liability for more serious or crippling injuries,[5] which invariably takes the form of a list of injuries followed by the penalty for each.[6] The injuries most commonly listed are eye,[7] bone,[8] hand,[9] foot[10] and tooth.[11] Slightly less common are nose[12] and ear.[13] Injuries that are truly unique to one code are few: finger (CE 43), burn (Ex. 21,25) and head-wound (HL 9).[14] We suspect that the injuries of $pṣ'$ and $ḥbwrh$ in Ex. 21,15, which are often used as a couplet and may even indicate hendiadys,[15] are parallel to the crushed limb of CU 16.[16] On the other hand, it is remarkable that two of the codes, CE 42 and CH

---

3 Text: YOS I 28. Translation: J.J. Finkelstein, ANET, p. 525.

4 In addition, the problem includes the case of an ox killing another ox, where the provisions of CE 54 and Ex. 21,35 are virtually identical.

5 Except in AL, where the provisions on miscarriage stand alone.This is because AL is organized differently from the other codes,being a series of tablets each with its own theme. Tablet A, where the miscarriage provisions are found, is reserved for laws connected with women.

6 Such a list was present in CU, but most of it, and the surrounding provisions, are lost. Likewise the relevant provisions of CL are not preserved, except for the miscarriage case on a fragment (UM-55-21-71) which may be associated with CL (referred to here as CL (Civil)). See M. Civil, "New Sumerian Law Fragments", AS 16, 4-6

7 CE 42, CH 196-199, HL 7, Ex. 21,24, Lev. 24,20. Cf. Dt. 19,21.

8 Or limb : CH 197, CU (15)-16, XII Tables 8,2-3, Lev. 24,20(šbr?).

9 CE 44, HL 11-12, Ex. 21,24, Lev. 24,20, cf. Dt. 19,21

10 CU 15, CE 45, HL 11-12, Ex. 21,24, cf. Dt. 19,21.

11 CU 19 (?), CH 200-201, HL 7, Ex. 21,24, Lev. 24,20, cf. Dt.19,21.

12 CU 17, CE 42, HL 13.

13 CE 42, HL 15.

14 See Haase, Bib. Or. 19(1962) 114-116.

15 See Koehler-Baumgartner 899 sub. $pṣ'$ and cf. Dt. 23,2.

16 gìr-pad-du ... in-zi-ir : JCS 22(1969) p. 70 lines 334-336.

202-205, should include with this repertory of physical injuries an injury to one's honour alone: slap in the face.

Thus the form of the lists, the close correlation of their contents and their association with cases 1 and 2 above make it unlikely that they are all coincidentally the same response to a familiar situation.[17]

Furthermore, to the Ancient Near Eastern provisions on this topic we would add the XII Tables from early Roman law, which we have already suggested derives from the cuneiform schools tradition. A fragment of the code preserves the remains of a very similar list:[18] crushed limb, broken bone, slap in the face.

On the other hand, when we consider the penalties imposed for causing death or injury, a fundamental dichotomy emerges in all except the first case, the unpremeditated blow resulting in only temporary injury. The codes fall into two groups. In the first, consisting of CH, AL, Exodus, and the XII Tables, there is heavy use of the death penalty and of corporal punishment, especially talionic, with recourse to money payments only secondarily in what were considered less serious cases. The second group - CU, CE and HL - by contrast knows nothing of the death penalty for such offences,[19] and nothing of corporal and talionic punishment; they lay down strictly pecuniary penalties in all cases.

This dichotomy has been the subject of great controversy and has led to a number of conflicting theories as to the nature of punishment in the Ancient Near Eastern legal systems.

II THEORIES OF PUNISHMENT

1. The classical theory[20] saw in the different penalties evidence of a general development in the law. In the earliest stage justice is a matter of revenge. Where a member of one family has killed or injured a member of another family, there will be a blood-feud between the two. The only relief was where the two sides agreed to composition, i.e. one side would acknowledge its guilt and buy off the other's revenge with an agreed payment.

The second stage is where the community lays down the rule that in the case of murder, death of the murderer is sufficient revenge and peace must then be restored. This is the germ of the talionic

---

17 The use of such a list out of context in Dt. 19,21 suggests a well-known formula.

18 Table VIII 2-4 : membrum ruptum, os fractum, iniuria. Ed. S.Riccobono, *Fontes Iuris Romani Anteiustiniani* Pt. I, Florence 1941, 53-54. See below under *Injury*.

19 CU has now been discovered to have the death penalty for premeditated murder. It appears separately at the very beginning of the code. See below.

20 For the best modern expression of this nineteenth-century view,see Driver and Miles, *The Babylonian Laws*, Vol. I 501-502.

principle, which is extended to personal injury as well. The talionic principle is therefore introduced as a limit on indiscriminate revenge.

The third stage is where talio is replaced by fixed payments. This represents a change in the purpose of the penalty, from revenge to the beginnings of the modern principle of compensation. Thus the primitive law of the Bible and the XII Tables is reformed in this manner by the Rabbis and the classical Roman jurists respectively.

The discovery of CH seemed to confirm this view of development: the talionic principle was upheld in a code that pre-dated the Bible. There was, however, one puzzling feature. CH in fact contained a mixed system: talionic punishment where the victim was an aristocrat (awīlum), but fixed payments where he was a commoner (muškēnum). Why should such a reform in the law be confined to the commoner?

2. The theory of progression from revenge via talio to compensation was upset by the discovery of still earlier codes than CH, namely CE and CU, in which the penalties for death and injury were strictly pecuniary. Accordingly, A.S. Diamond proposed the opposite theory of development:[21] there is a universal progression in law from pecuniary sanctions to corporal ones. It represents a sociological advance in the perception of wrongs from civil to criminal, as the power and influence of the State increases.

The idea of a universal progression creates some difficulties for the theory. For example, Diamond is forced to dismiss apparently early references to talio in Exodus in the XII Tables as later interpolations.[22] Moreover, the Hittite Laws, which are later than CH and AL, nonetheless contain pecuniary and not corporal sanctions. Diamond's explanation here is that the progression is sociological, not chronological, the Babylonian and Assyrian States being more advanced in terms of centralized power.[23]

3. J.J. Finkelstein produced a refinement of the same theory, arguing that talio represented an advance in jurisprudential rather than sociological terms.[24] The idea of physical punishment for physical injuries was an innovation in CH, replacing the earlier practice of treating physical assaults, including homicide, as private civil invasions remediable by pecuniary satisfaction. It represents an enlargement of the scope of criminal law which

---

21 "An Eye for an Eye", Iraq 19(1957) 151-155.

22 Ibid., 153.

23 Ibid., 155.

24 "Ammiṣaduqa's Edict and the Babylonian 'Law Codes'", JCS 15 (1961) 91-104, at 96-99.

prefers the aristocrat over the commoner, since physical invasions against the former are raised to the status of crimes and therefore punishable by a public authority, while the latter must remain content with mere civil damages.

4. Finkelstein's theory has been adopted by a school of biblical scholars, which holds that the Bible represents an even greater advance, since the protection of *talio* is extended to all members of society (except for slaves), thus ensuring equitable justice: the rich receive the same punishment as the poor.[25]

5. The leading school of thought, therefore, is that the difference between the codes with pecuniary and those with physical penalties can be explained as a process whereby the latter come to replace the former. We find this explanation unacceptable for two main reasons: Firstly, the chronological approach espoused by Diamond and Finkelstein is unsatisfactory. The pecuniary penalties appear sometimes in early laws and sometimes in late laws: in order to fit them into the desired chronology value judgments must be made on the level of "civilization" represented by the code in question. But how does it come about that CH represents a civilized society, while CE, promulgated a short distance away and not much more than thirty years earlier, is still "barbaric"?[26] Or indeed is the Sumerian culture represented by CU and so admired by the Babylonians - so much so that copies of CU continued to be made in the Old Babylonian period - equally barbaric? The same applies to the Hittites, and perhaps even more so, since they almost certainly had had the privilege of reading CH[27] and could not therefore be accused of ignorance in the realm of jurisprudential advances.

Secondly, the theory is based on a totally false conception of the relationship between criminal and civil law. In modern legal systems there is a sharp distinction between these two branches of the law. In the former, the interests of the community as a whole are at stake : initiative is therefore in the hands of the State and the purpose is to punish the offender, not to indemnify the victim. The benefit to the victim lies in the deterrent power of the

---

25 S. Paul, *Studies in the Book of the Covenant*, Leiden 1970, 75-77,and the authors cited at p.77 n.4.

26 Finklestein's term, reversing an application of the same by Kraus to talionic punishment : *ibid.* p. 98. T. Frymer-Kensky ("Tit for Tat" *BA* 43 (1980) 230-234) suggests that talionic punishment is of West Semitic Origin. But she herself notes that the idea appears in a Sumerian code (CL 25). Further problems with this view are the apparent absence of the talionic idea from CE and HL, which might be thought to be under West Semitic rather than Sumerian influence.

27 G.Cardascia, "La Transmission des sources juridiques cunéiformes", *RIDA* 7(1960) 43-50, and Westbrook, "Biblical and Cuneiform Law Codes", *RB* 92 (1985) p.256.

punishment, but of course for the victim in the particular case it comes too late. The civil law, on the other hand, is concerned with the interests of the individual : initiative is in the hands of the victim himself and the purpose is compensation.[28]

Even in modern law, however, the two categories *are not mutually exclusive*. The same act, if it infringes the interests of both the individual and the State, will at the same time constitute both a tort and a crime. The thief, assailant and murderer are punished by criminal law, but this does not prevent the victim from suing the offender for conversion, assault or wrongful death.[29]

The claim that in the ancient systems, therefore, physical penalties represented an advance and even a privilege would not be true if they came to *replace* compensation rather than to supplement it. If the deterrent power of the physical punishment fails, as it often will, the victim will have suffered permanent injury and receive no compensation therefor. The knowledge that his attacker will suffer the same fate may indeed give moral satisfaction, but on its own it is a poor remedy.

Moreover, the very distinction between punishment and compensation is anachronistic and does not apply to Ancient Near Eastern Law. The existence of multiple damages for theft - a

---

28 Even in modern systems the distinction is stricter in theory than in practice: in English Law, for example, private prosecuion is still widely used for offences such as shoplifting (by large stores who wish to publicize a deterrent), while in civil suits "exemplary"or "punitive" damages are sometimes possible. In American law this is so "especially where the defendant's wrongdoing has been intentional and deliberate, and has the character of outrage frequently associated with crime..." : Prosser, *Law of Torts* 4th ed., St. Paul Minn., 1971, p. 9.

29 "The same act may be both a crime against the state and a tort against an individual. In such a case, since the interests invaded are not the same, and the objects to be accomplished by the two suits are different, there may be both a civil tort action and a criminal prosecution for the same offense." Prosser, *ibid*, p. 7. This position is axiomatic among lawyers of the Common Law, the only exclusionary element being a procedural one, and this not shared by all systems: "If the crime is a felony, it was the law in England that the tort is so far "merged" in the crime that the civil action must be suspended or stayed until the criminal one had been completed... Early American decisions took over the rule, but it has now been almost entirely discarded in the United States." Prosser, *ibid*. p.8.

In French law, the injured party actually has the option of bringing a separate civil action in the civil courts or of attaching it to the criminal procedure. See J.C. Soyer, *Droit Pénale et Procedure Pénale* 5th ed., Paris 1977, paras. 429-440. For a restatement of the complementary nature of tort and crime in French law, see *ibid*. para 395.

The only major system we know that denies a civil remedy where criminal punishment has been imposed for the same offence is Jewish(i.e. Rabbinic) Law, but there it is a late development, post-Tannaitic at least as regards the death penalty and even later in its general formulation. See B. Lifshitz, "'Does a Man Not Receive Both the Death Penalty and Pay Damages?' (On the Question of the Origin of the Rule "Kom leh Miderabah Mineh")", *Shenaton Ha-Mishpat Ha-Ivri* 8(1981) 153-246. (In Hebrew).

supposedly private claim by the owner - demonstrates that monetary payments were not regarded as morally neutral. There is no reason therefore to regard the fixed payments required by some law codes for personal injury as pure indemnification.

6. To explain why some laws impose physical punishment while others in the same circumstances prescribe only pecuniary penalties, we would take as our starting-point the perceptive surmise of U. Cassuto that in cases where talionic punishment was prescribed, there nonetheless existed the alternative of ransom: "Theoretically, he who blinds another's eye should be sentenced to have his own blinded; only he is permitted to give a ransom in order to save his eye."[30]

We would propose the following hypothesis:

(a) It was accepted throughout the Ancient Near East that injury or killing gave rise to a right to revenge by the victim and/or his family on the perpetrator and/or his family. It was equally accepted that that same right could be commuted into a money payment, i.e. that revenge could be bought off with a ransom.

(b) This dual right - to revenge or ransom - was a legal right - that is to say, it was enforceable with the aid of the machinery of the legal system. In order to enforce the right, however, the law had first to define its limits.

(c) Where the rule of law did not prevail - because there was no civilized society or no effective State - the right would be not legal but at the most moral, and enforcement would be by self-help. Equally,the limits on the right would not be legal, but emotional or practical.This was not the case, it must be emphasized, in the Ancient Near East,where civilized society had existed for hundreds of years before the appearance of the first legal records, where the States from which our records derive in general had effective legal systems,[31] and wherethere even existed a recognized system of international law to cover offences beyond the boundaries of the individual States.

On the other hand, these societies did assume that in the absence of the rule of law, the right to revenge would exist in the form described above. Two passages from the Bible are indicative of this point.

Firstly, there is the boast of Lamech in Gen. 4,23-4: "For I have slain a man for a wound on me, a boy for a blow on me. Cain shall be avenged sevenfold, but Lamech seventy-sevenfold". The second passage is the account of Samson's revenge on the Philistines for

---

30 *A Commentary on the Book of Exodus,* Jerusalem 1967, 276-277(English translation).

31 With the obvious exception of periods where there was a breakdown in authority due to war, civil disturbance, etc.

the wrong that his betrothed's father had done him[32] (Jud. 15,1-8), which consists of burning their crops and committing a great slaughter among them.[33]

In both cases, revenge is enforced by self-help and limited only by the avenger's discretion. The situation described is that which existed before the rule of law but it is not evidence of real historical development. If such a stage of lawlessness ever existed, it is lost in the realms of pre-history. The two passages are evidence of psychological history : they are legends describing what was *perceived* to have been the unsatisfactory situation before the advent of civilized society : Lamech lived before the Flood and Samson in what was seen as a period of anarchy: when "each man did what was right in his own eyes".[34]

(d) In practice, as opposed to legend, therefore, revenge was regulated by law. On what criteria? The most obvious principle of justice is that the revenge should in some way be commensurate with the hurt caused. The talionic formula is but one expression of this principle. It is an ideal, and not always appropriate as we shall see, for the "proper" revenge was sometimes considered to be more than strict *talio*, and sometimes less.

(e) It is not only the right to revenge which is regulated, but also its counterpart, the right to ransom. Where revenge is limited, it will tend to have a limiting effect on the amount of ransom that can be demanded in lieu. But some of the law-codes were not content with this indirect influence; they intervened directly to regulate the ransom itself. The lists of fixed payments for death or injury are another facet of that cardinal activity of the law-codes: price-fixing.

Fixing the price of ransom, however, does not altogether exclude the possibility of revenge; the victim's right retained its dual aspect.What it does do is to make the right to revenge a residuary right. The choice of ransom is shifted from the avenger to the offender, for only if the offender fails to pay is the right of revenge operable. Were it otherwise, price-fixing would be a two-edged sword: limiting the ransom would make revenge overly attractive.

The law-codes sometimes regulate the aspect of revenge and sometimes the aspect of ransom, but in either case the unexpressed

---

32 In giving his bride to the best man, which is forbidden in several cuneiform law codes. See A. Van Selms, "The Best Man and Bride -From Sumer to St. John", *JNES* 9(1950) 65-75.

33 See Chapter Three.

34 Cf. Jacobsen's remarks on Mesopotamian perception of the difference between barbarism and civilization in *The Harab Myth*,Sources from the Ancient Near East Vol 2, fasc. 3, Malibu 1984, p.17: "... in so far as it (the myth) shows a gradual change from primitive barbarous licentiousness to the existing world order it is a history of cosmic morals."

assumption is that the other aspect still exists as an alternative.

This is our hypothesis. We now turn to consider the evidence of the sources.

III. PUNISHMENT IN THE SOURCES

(A) Homicide

1. Death Penalty

The only paragraph of a cuneiform law code so far recovered that deals directly with murder is CU (Yildiz) 1.[35] It reads, in Yildiz' translation: "If a man commits murder, that man is to be killed."[36]

A death sentence for premeditated murder is also recorded in the Nippur Murder Trial,[37] which further reveals the ideology behind it and some details of the procedure. Lines 30-34 read: "As men who have killed men they are not live men; the males (all) three of them and that woman before the chair of PN (the victim) shall be killed". And it is recorded at the end of the trial (which is concerned not directly with the murder but with a legal point: the liability of an accessory after the fact) that the guilty persons "were delivered up to be killed."

Our third source is an angry letter from the King of Babylon to the Egyptian Pharoah:[38] "...In the city of Hinnatuni in the land of Canaan, A and B from the city of Akko sent their men and killed my merchants and took their money.... Canaan is your land and its kings are your servants. I have been robbed in your land! Bind them and restore in full the money that they took. And the men who killed my servants - kill them. Return their blood!"

At first sight these three sources - two from the Old Babylonian and one from the Middle Babylonian period[39] - seem unequivocal. The penalty for murder is death; it is a public matter in which the victim's family is not involved; still less is there any hint of ransom. Closer attention to the details, however, reveals a number

35 The biblical law codes' provisions on murder will be discussed separately in the final section.

36 *Or.* 50 (1981) p. 95.

37 Edited by T. Jacobsen, "An Ancient Mesopotamian Trial for Homicide" in *Toward the Image of Tammuz*, Harvard Semitic Series Vol. 21, Cambridge Mass. 1970, 193-214.

38 El-Amarna No 8. Ed. J.A. Knudtzon, *Die El-Amarna-Tafeln* VAB 11, Pt.I, Leipzig 1908, 85-89.

39 All these sources have a significance beyond their own time and place. The two Sumerian documents exist only in Old Babylonian copies, showing their continued influence, and the El-Amarna letter comes from the sphere of international relations, demonstrating that a common idea of the nature of murder and the appropriate penalty existed among the states of the area.

of contrary indications.

Let us begin with the Nippur trial. It is not stated who brought the charges or who carried out the sentence, and Jacobsen speculates that there may have been a specific "criminal" procedural tradition of communal action to prevent pollution of the community by the crime.[40] None of this is in the text, however; the only positive indication that it contains points in a different direction, as Jacobsen notes:[41] "The...statement...ordering the death penalty and specifying that it is to be imposed in front of the chair of the slain....constitutes one of the very few survivals of the concept of blood revenge to be found in older Mesopotamian sources: the thirst for personal revenge in the soul of the slain man is to be assuaged by the killing of his slayer before his chair, that is symbolically, in his presence."

We would suggest that this statement was no mere survival of blood revenge but an indication of how the death penalty was generally conceived. The revenge in question, moreover, had a concrete as well as a metaphysical form. Again, we may follow Jacobsen's analysis:[42] "The phrasing of the statement which records the commitment of the condemned into the hands of their executioners gives no indication who these were. The term used, sum: "to deliver up", "to hand over", "to give", is used in records of civil trials of the awarding of a disputed object to the winning party by the court or - with the losing party as object - of the awarding of a right *in personam*.

We suggest that the procedure here was no different: the condemned murderers were handed over to the plaintiffs in the case, who, as we shall see presently, would be relatives of the victim. And as to the execution, Jacobsen continues:[43] "As our document gives no indication of who executed the verdict of death, so do the codes known to us use only noncommittal expressions such as "he/she/they shall be killed" or "they shall kill them". Who "they" in the latter case are is not stated."

In the text before us, the Sumerian verb translated "shall be killed" is ì-gaz-dè-èš, which would more literally be translated "they shall kill (them)". The same active verbal form is found in CU (Yildiz) 1: ì-gaz-e-dam. The literal translation would

---

40 Based on the evidence from three early myths : op.cit. 204-207. None of these involve murder, however, and in one, "The Guilty Slavegirl," it is the injured party - her mistress - who pronounces the death sentence.

41 *Ibid.* p.209.

42 *Ibid.* p.214.

43 *Loc. cit.*

therefore be "he shall kill (the murderer)". The death sentence is not impersonal; it is in the hands of a person too well known to the ancient authors to bear express mention, but still hidden from us.

The circumstances of the El-Amarna letter make the identity of the plaintiff clear, at least. The Babylonian king regards himself as having been robbed and the murder of his servants as an injury to himself. He therefore demands compensation for the goods stolen, but it may be presumed that the compensation will go to the merchants' families rather than to the king personally.[44] The same may be deduced for the destination of the blood to be "returned". In view of the international character of the case and the privileged position of the merchants, the king takes upon himself the role of plaintiff and expects the Pharoah to act as his agent in the matter of execution.

If the three sources above reveal that the death sentence is a form of revenge, the question arises of the limits on that revenge. The role of the court is seen to lie in determining liability and in providing the machinery whereby those liable are delivered into the hands of the avengers, but there is no express mention of its regulatory function. Nonetheless, it is to be noted that in all three cases only the persons directly connected with the murder, and not their families, are to be executed, and CU (Yildiz) 1 contains a hint that this is not self-evident: lú-bi ì-gaz-e-dam "he shall kill *that man*".

There remains the question of ransom, and here at least, the silence of these three documents cannot be broken. For evidence of the alternative of ransom, we must turn to other sources.

2. The Choice of Death or Ransom

The clearest expression of the choice that the avenger of the murdered man has is given in the Edict of Telipinus 49:[45]

A matter of blood is as follows. Whoever does blood, whatever the owner of the blood says:- If he says "Let him die!" he shall die. If he says "Let him compensate!" he shall compensate. But to the king, nothing.

It needs no special exegesis of our literal translation to conclude that bloodshed is at issue, and the "owner of the blood" is the person with the right to revenge. What is less clear, however, is the purpose of this paragraph.

In our view, it does not introduce a new rule on the penalty for

---

44 Similar provisions are found in treaties from Ugarit dealing with the robbery and murder of foreign merchants. See below.

45 Edited by I.Hoffman, *Der Erlass Telipinus*, Heidelberg 1964, 52-3.

murder but restates the traditional position, which is incidental to its main purpose. That purpose is revealed by the laconic closing phrase. The Telipinus-Edict is a reform text, and one of the traditional features of royal reforms, which is apparent in the Hittite Laws also, is the abolition of paymeets due to the king.[46] Thus whatever choice the avenger makes, the traditional payment to the king (for the services of the royal courts in bringing the culprit to justice?) is dispensed with.[47]

The same principle of choice is reiterated in AL 'B' 2:

> If one of undivided brothers has taken a life, they shall give him to the owner of the life. If he chooses, the owner of the life may kill him; if he chooses, he shall make composition and take his share.

Again, the avenger's choice is incidental to the main point of the law. The period between the death of a householder and division of the inheritance by his sons gives rise to difficulties in law, since the brothers hold the estate jointly, and thus can be said to be at the same time owners of the whole or nothing. Theoretically, then, the "owner of the life" could claim the whole estate as ransom for the killer's life, which would be unfair to the other brothers. This rule therefore limits his potential ransom to the equivalent of a single share in the estate. It also assumes that vengeance must be confined to the killer himself, seeking on the same principle to prevent liability for the ransom from spilling over on to the brothers.[48]

Evidence that the choice operated in practice is provided by a Neo-Assyrian contract. ADD 321[49] reads:

> [Beginning broken]...[50] A son of B shall give C the slave-woman, the daughter of D, the scribe, together with her family, in lieu of the blood. He shall wash the blood.[51]

---

46 E.g. HL 9. See also M. Weinfeld, *Justice and Righteousness in Israel and the Nations*, Jerusalem 1985, chapter 4.

47 Our interpretation follows that of Hoffman, op.cit. 81-82. See already V. Korosec, "La Codification dans le Domaine du Droit Hittite", *RIDA* 4(1957) 102-103.

48 A similar phrase occurs in AL 'A'10, but the context is too broken for any valid conclusions to be drawn.

49 See the edition of Kohler-Ungnad, *Assyrische Rechtsurkunden*, Leipzig 1913, no.659.

50 There is possibly a reference to the ordeal: [ ] ..ma-a it-ta-at-ru-uṣ. The phrase *huršāna tarāṣu* means 'to undergo the ordeal': AHw 1326, mng. 7b.

51 It is not clear whether this is the effect of the payment or a separate act. We incline to the latter view, since contractual clauses do not usually explain their effect. Perhaps it refers to an expiatory sacrifice that the guilty party must bring to assuage the gods, or to ritual cleansing of the place where the crime was committed. See note 57 below.

If he does not give the woman, they will kill him on top of B's grave.[52] Whoever among them reneges upon the contract[53] [will pay] 10 mina of silver. (Oath, witnesses, date).

Once the parties have negotiated the amount of ransom, therefore, the agreement is framed as a simple contract. The only difference is that non-performance, i.e. non-payment of the ransom, leads to revival of the original right to revenge, surrender of which was the quid pro quo of the ransom.

Further evidence of practice comes from the Bible. King Saul had had large numbers of the Gibeonites killed, an act which was deemed murder because it had been in breach of a treaty.[54] In 2 S. 21,1-9, David offers to compensate (kpr) them for the crime. The Gibeonites immediately understand this to mean that Saul's family will be forced to pay a ransom (v. 4: "we have no claim[55] of silver or gold against Saul and his house"), but prefer to exercise their right to revenge. David's role is that of a court of law: the court's task is to determine the appropriate measure of revenge in the circumstances (which David does by acquiescing in the Gibeonites' proposal) and to hand over those liable to vengeance into the hands of the avengers.

In the cuneiform sources we have seen that the avenger is identified only as the 'owner of the blood/life'.[56] The case of the Gibeonites shows the avengers to be at least members of the same clan. A letter from the Hittite king Hattusili III to the Babylonian king Kadašman-Enlil II concerning the procedures in a case of murder[57] mentions the victim's brothers[58] in this role. For the

---

52 The significance of the place of execution being the payor's father's grave is not clear. Perhaps B was the father of the victim and the killer, i.e. a crime between brothers, as in 2 S. 14,1-11. Kohler-Ungnad try to solve the problem by making A the payee, but this assumes a dative preposition which is not in the text.

53 This refers to a later denial of the contract's validity, not to non-performance (which can only apply to A) which is dealt with in the preceding clause.

54 And therefore was not a legitimate act of warfare. M. Greenberg ("Some Postulates of Biblical Criminal Law", Yehezkel Kaufmann Jubilee Volume, Jerusalem 1960, p.24) appears to suggest that the death sentence was for breach of the treaty oath made in the name of God. In that case, divine punishment or punishment by the whole community without reference to the murders would have been expected. The procedure followed and the Gibeonites' concern is connected with the killings, not with the oath violation as such, which is mentioned only as an explanatory gloss (v.2). God's own explanation refers to murder and not to the treaty (v.1).

55 The Hebrew phrase lnw 'm PN is parallel to the Babylonian ina muhhi PN išû and the Assyrian ina pāni PN išû 'to have a debt-claim against someone'.

56 See also ADD 164, discussed below.

57 KBo I 10 Rs 15-26. The left-hand side of the column is broken at this point, making it difficult to follow the thread of the king's argument. We disagree with H. Klengel's restoration ("Mord und Busseleistung in spätbronzezeitlichen Syrien" in
(continued on the next page)

closest definition, however, we must return to the Bible, where the avenger is called the 'redeemer of the blood'.[59] 'Redeemer' in the law of inheritance refers to an agnate of the subject of redemption, who is a potential heir to the latter's estate and at the same time has various rights (e.g. redemption of that estate) and duties (levirate) vis-à-vis the latter. In default of a brother, the role of redeemer will pass to the next agnate in line, in the same way as inheritance.[60]

Consequently, the three sources in the preceding section should be read in the light of the above evidence. In the Nippur murder trial, it is not the State which prosecutes and executes, as in a modern criminal trial, but it is the court which determines guilt, the appropriate revenge, and then hands those liable over to the victim's relatives for revenge. The fact that no ransom is mentioned in the case is due to the avengers' prior exercise of their choice in the matter, like the Gibeonites. The same applies to the Babylonian king's letter to the Pharaoh, whose angry tone suggests

Death in Mesopotamia ed. B. Alster, Copenhagen 1980), which confuses murder and execution. In particular, the letter cannot be interpreted as stating that the death penalty does not exist in Hatti, nor that the alternative to ransom for murder is slavery (Klengel's restoration, nowhere else attested). We would very tentatively translate and restore as follows:

15-16. ..as to what you wrote to me, saying "My merchants are being murdered in the land of Amurru, of Ugarit (and of ...), no-one is being murdered in the land of Hatti.

17-18 (Should) a person be murdered, if the king hears [he investigates] that matter [and if] the murderer is caught [he is handed over] to the brothers of the murdered man.

19-20/ If the brothers take ransom-money (*kasap mullê*) for the murdered man [they release] the murderer [...and...] they purify the place of the murder.

/20-22/ If the brothers will not accept [ransom-mon]ey they may [kill (=*damê epē šu*??)] the murderer.

/22-23/ If a man has committed a crime against a king and [flees] to another land [he is arrested / extradited/given asylum]; it is not the practice to murder him.

/23 My brother, ask and they will tell you.

24 [...] those who would not murder a rebel, would they murder a merchant?

25/ As for the Subarians, how would I know if they are committing murder?

/25-26 Now send the brothers of the murdered merchant to me and I will examine their case.

58 This term is not as clear-cut as it looks; it could refer to unspecified relatives, or even colleagues in a guild, in the case of a merchant.

59 *g'l hdm*: Num. 35, 19.21.25.27; Dt. 19, 6.12; Jos.20,3.5.9; 2 S. 14,11.

60 See Westbrook, "Redemption of Land", *ILR* 6(1971) 370, 375, and "The Biblical Law of Levirate", *RIDA* 24 (1977) 65-87. Phillips (*Ancient Israel's Criminal Law*, 102-106) argues that the 'redeemer of blood' is not to be identified with the 'redeemer', i.e. the nearest kinsman, but is a technical expression for an official designated by the murderer's city to inflict execution on their behalf. The difficulty with this view is that in Num 35,12 'redeemer' alone is used of the avenger of blood. Phillips overcomes this difficulty (*JJS* 28(1977)111) by assuming the Massoretic text to be incorrect. Assumptions of this nature were better applied to the modern theory than to the ancient text.

that ransom was not acceptable.

Even the laconic terms of CU(Yildiz) 1 can yield to this interpretation. The Sumerian verb translated "he shall kill" could equally well be translated "he may kill", i.e. giving the avenger the right to kill the murderer. Once it is seen as a right, then it may be commuted into ransom.

We would not, however, place too much emphasis on the form of the verb. If the accepted method of dealing with homicide is revenge or ransom, and the law intervenes for the purpose of regulating this system, then the penalty applicable can be expressed in many ways, even in absolute terms, without derogating from the alternatives known to exist. Indeed, when we look at the phrasing of the death penalty in the Ancient Near Eastern law codes, we find a bewildering variety.

CE does not refer to killing at all; the equivalent phrase is *imât* 'he shall die' or *imât ul iballuṭ* 'he shall die; he shall not live'. CH has two forms: *iddâk* 'he shall be killed' and *idukkū* 'they shall kill (him)', while AL has the latter form only. The biblical codes have *(mwt) ymwt/ywmt* 'he shall (surely) die / be caused to die'.

As regards the cuneiform codes,[61] two of the above phrases have been the subject of analysis, and the result is a salutary warning to those who would mechanically impose modern penal conceptions upon ancient law. The phrase 'he shall die; he shall not live' in CE seems peremptory indeed, and has been taken to indicate a mandatory death sentence.[62] Yaron has pointed out,[63] however, that a far more satisfactory explanation arises from the context in which this particular phrase occurs: it excuses spontaneous reaction by the aggrieved party e.g. in killing a thief caught breaking in at night.

The use of two different forms in CH has been explained by Driver and Miles as follows:[64] *iddâk* refers to execution by the State; *idukkū* to execution by way of private vengeance. This distinction, however, is difficult to apply to the substantive law of the code. Why, for example, should a person who hides a runaway slave be subject to public execution (16,19), while one who suborns a barber to remove a slave's mark so that he cannot be traced, be subject to private revenge (227)? More significantly, why should the builder be executed when his negligence has caused a householder's death (229), but his son be the object of revenge when the same negligence causes a son's death (230)? Driver and Miles

---

61 For the biblical codes, see the discussion in the final section of this chapter.
62 See E. Szlechter, *Les Lois d'Ešnunna*, Paris 1954, 110-111.
63 *The Laws of Eshnunna*, p. 173.
64 *The Babylonian Laws*, Vol.I, 494-498.

explain the latter case as follows: "If the owner is killed, there might be no one able to avenge him, so that the state inflicts the penalty; but, if the son is killed, the owner and his kin will kill the son of the builder."[65] But we see no reason why the kin of the owner should not be able to act in the first instance, as we have seen is the case in some of the examples discussed above.

We would suggest a different approach. Jacobsen has observed that the term lú/*awīlum* in the Mesopotamian law-codes, although it can generally be translated 'man', 'person', refers essentially to the head of a household.[66] If the law wishes to specify that the subject or object of the rule is a subordinate member of the household, it will give their status, e.g. wife, son, daughter or slave. There is nothing remarkable in this : even in modern systems the archetypal legal personality is the householder.[67]

If we look at the terminology for capital and corporal punishment in CH, we see that the normal form is the indefinite third person plural, which is applied indifferently to the head and to subordinate members of the household ("they shall burn, throw in the water", etc.).

The passive form *iddâk*, on the other hand, applies exclusively to the head of household, expressly called an *awīlum* or impliedly so.[68] The only exception is one that proves the rule : the taverness (*sabītum*) in 109, who, unlike the wife or daughter, is a woman *sui iuris*. The distinction is clearest in the case of the builder discussed above: when the penalty falls on the builder himself, it is expressed by *iddâk*; when it falls upon his son, it is expressed by *idukkū*. Of the five cases in the Code where *iddukū* is used, three refer to a subordinate member of the household - son or daughter.[69] In the two other cases, the object is an *awīlum*, but a multiple verb is used: *idukkūšūma ihallalūšu*.[70] The distinction may therefore be stylistic rather than legal, since the passive form is never used in the Code in conjunction with another verb.[71]

65 *Ibid.*, p. 498.

66 In an oral communication. Cf. *ibid.*, *Essays in Memory of J.J. Finkelstein*, 115-116.

67 Cf. the French legal term "bon père de famille".

68 In paragraph 9 he is called simply 'the seller', but para. 12 reveals him to be a head of household. Para. 26, soldier; paras 33-34, officer; para. 229, builder.

69 116, 120, 230.

70 21, 227.

71 This would account for the change in the form of *dâku* for the taverness in 108: "they shall convict her and throw her in the water". In fact the second part of the phrase is so standard - being taken from a penalty-clause upon the wife in marriage contracts - that the scribe in 155 used the feminine accusative pronominal suffix in error, forgetting that the object of the verb was a man, and a head of household to boot.

The legal reason behind this stylistic difference is not clear,[72] but it does indicate how important the status of the parties is in the matter of punishment.

3. Vicarious Punishment

a) The idea of mitigation

Where the penalty for an act by the head of household falls not upon himself but upon a subordinate member of his family, it is considered a mitigated form of punishment upon the head of household. Thus in the case of the poor man's ewe-lamb, God informs David that he has reduced the original death sentence upon David to a death-sentence upon his son.[73] David regards the sentence as a punishment imposed upon himself.[74]

In the law codes, the lighter penalty of vicarious punishment is sometimes applied in cases of non-premeditated homicide, but sometimes it is demonstratively not applied. HL 43-44a read:

If a man customarily fords a river with his ox and another pushes him aside, seizes the tail of the ox and crosses the river, but the river carries the owner of the ox away, they shall take that very man.

If someone pushes a man into a fire and he dies, he (the offender) shall give to him a son/heir.[75]

Two cases of non-premeditated homicide are presented. In neither was it the direct intention of the offender to kill: in the case of the river, it was to cross and in the case of the fire, probably only to wound.[76] Nonetheless, it was reasonably foreseeable that

---

72 We doubt that it lies in the mode of execution. In two other paragraphs where the passive is used, the circumstances are diametrically opposite. In 25, the looter of a burning house is thrown into the fire - a case of lynch justice (inaddî). In 204 one who slaps a superior's face is whipped a set number of times before the Assembly (immahhaṣ) - a formal procedure. The passive form may refer to the fact that the court is directly responsible for handing over the guilty head of household, but only indirectly responsible for the subordinate (it forces the head of household to hand him over). On the other hand, the 3rd person plural is commonly used with a head of household as object.

73 2 S. 12, 13-15.

74 Ibid v. 22. Cf. the case of Ahab 1 K. 21,27-9.

75 Restoring D[UMU].NI[TA]-an.

76 Death was not the inevitable result of being pushed into the fire: presumably a small hearth fire is meant rather than a blazing inferno. There is also the element of indirect causation in these two cases, in that it is the water and the fire that do the killing. We would not place too much emphasis on this factor, however. We have seen in the previous chapter that indirect causation as such (King David's killing of Uriah by the sword of the Ammonites) does not remove liability. For a case where killing a person by the agency of fire provided no excuse, cf. King Rim-Sin of Larsa's ruling: "Because he threw the boy into the oven, you throw the slave into the furnace." (BIN 7,10 : 7-10).

death could ensue and the offender is judged by this objective standard.[77] In 43, the offender's act is considered of sufficient gravity for the penalty to fall upon himself, as in premeditated murder; 'they shall take that very man' means that the relatives of the deceased are entitled to take revenge upon the offender himself.[78] In 44a, the circumstances were apparently less culpable, and accordingly the offender may hand over his son for revenge as a mitigated punishment of himself.

For another example of the application and non-application of mitigation, we return to the case of the negligent builder in CH 229-231:

> If a builder builds a house for a man and does not make his work strong and the house that he built falls down and causes the householder's death, that builder shall be put to death. If it causes the death of the householder's son, they shall put to death that builder's son. If it causes the death of the householder's slave, he shall give the householder slave for slave.

If the same act of negligence by the builder as head of household kills a head of household, revenge is allowed upon the builder himself; if it kills only a son, revenge is limited to his son; if it kills a slave, he must replace him with a slave of his own. The principle here is talionic, but this is not the point of the law. The builder's *mens rea* is a mitigating factor, being negligence rather than intent, and accordingly a small concession is made where the victim is a subordinate member of the household.

The same applies in CH 116, where a creditor causes the death of a distrainee through blows or ill-treatment.[79] It was not his intention to kill, but he should have foreseen the possibility, and a mitigated penalty is imposed; if the victim is only a son, revenge is limited to the offender's son.

---

77 Cf. the vacillations of English law on the question of objective liability for murder. In *D.P.P. v. Smith* [1961] AC 290, D did not intend to kill, but a reasonable man would have realized that his unlawful act was likely, in the circumstances, to cause death. He was held guilty of murder. The decision caused an outcry, but to date has only been partly amended by legislation towards a more "subjective" test of *mens rea*. (See Smith and Hogan, *Criminal Law*, 5th ed., London 1983, 73, 295-296.)

78 A. Goetze provides a gloss to his translation (*ANET* (3rd ed.) 191 n.9): "i.e. the authorities of the respective village or town", without offering any evidence for this interpretation. This interpretation is all the more remarkable since one version has the verb in the singular (KBo VI 5, col.IV 15). The singular or plural can be used indifferently of the avenging family, but not of a public authority. Note also the change in the verb form between 43 and 44a: they *take* the head of household, but the head of household *gives* his son. Cf. note 72 above.

79 "If the distrainee dies in the distrainor's house through beating or maltreatment, the master of the distrainee shall prove it against his creditor (lit.:"merchant") and: if he was the man's son, they shall kill his son, if he was the man's slave, he shall pay one-third of a mina of silver. He shall forfeit as much as he gave."

In more culpable circumstances, however, the same principle negates the possibility of vicarious punishment. In CE 24 the creditor has likewise caused the death of a distrainee who is a subordinate member of the household (wife or son), but the distraint itself was unjustified.[80] Consequently, the revenge is expressly stated not to be vicarious - this is the import of the curious phrase "the distrainor who distrained shall die", which expresses the same idea as "they shall take that very man" in HL 43.

On the basis of our earlier discussion we would argue that in all these examples of vicarious (or non-vicarious) punishment the unspoken assumption was that the revenge could be replaced by ransom. Where the revenge is on a subordinate member of the household only, the ransom that can be demanded will tend to be less. This perhaps answers the question that is often raised about vicarious *talio* : what if the offender has no son?[81] The problem is less acute if a monetary payment can always be substituted, and the price-fixing of ransom that we shall see below may have arisen in order to deal with complications such as this.[82]

b) The goring ox

Explicit evidence on the role of ransom in vicarious *talio* comes from a classic school case of homicide by indirect causation : the goring ox. Before entering into a discussion of the substantive law, however, we must first clarify a point of terminology already adumbrated in our remarks on the status of the parties.

In the provisions of CH on injuries (206-214) and death by a goring ox (250-252), the term *mār awīlim,*: "son of a man", frequently occurs. In other parts of the Code the expression undoubtedly has its literal meaning,[83] but in these provisions commentators have preferred to attribute a different meaning: "member of the *awīlum*-class" (i.e. the aristocracy).[84] The reason seems to be that, in spite of the difficulties involved in attributing a double meaning to the term, there is no satisfactory explanation for the sudden appearance of a son in these provisions. In the light

---

80 "If he had nothing upon him, but distrained the wife of a *muškēnum*, the son of a *muškēnum* holds the distrainee in his house and caused their death, a case of life. The distrainer who distrained shall die."

81 E.g. by Finkelstein, *The Ox That Gored*, Transactions of the American Philosophical Society Vol 71 Pt. 2 (Philadelphia, 1981) p. 34.

82 The problem is considered explictly in the case of slaves : CU 21b, CL 13.

83 E.g. 7,14, 116.

84 Driver and Miles, *The Babylonian Laws* Vol. I p. 87, Meek, ANET p.175, F.R. Kraus, *Vom mesopotamischen Menschen der altbabylonischen Zeit und seiner Welt*, Amsterdam 1973, pp. 69, 98.

of our discussion above we would argue that there is, and that *mār* *(awīlim)* in all these provisions can only be translated "son of..." In this we are not relying solely on *a priori* reasoning from our own understanding of the law; the evidence lies in the formal structure of the Code.

As a work of "scientific" literature, CH deals with problems in the classic manner of Babylonian science: it considers what the solution would be in a standard set of variables. In this case the variables are where the victim is a head of household, a son (or daughter), and a slave. For example, CH 206-214 discusses the consequences of a blow in an affray and goes through a sequence of victims: 1) head of household *(awīlum)*: 206, 2) son *(mār* *awīlim/muškēnim)*: 207-208,[85] 3) daughter *(mārat awīlim/ muškē* *nim)*, where the term must refer to a daughter and not to a member of a class because of the provision for vicarious talio: 209-212, 4) slave: 213-214. Sometimes a second set of alternatives with some other element affecting the legal result - such as the circumstances or the consequences of the act - is imposed upon the first. This can be seen in the above sequence, (miscarriage/death of pregnant woman) and again in CH 115-116. Upon the standard set of variables as to status is imposed the set 'no liability/liability'. Thus, 1) the natural death of a distrainee affords no cause of action: 115,[86] 2) death by blows leads to talionic punishment if the distrainee is a son: 116, 3) the same leads to a fixed payment if the distrainee is a slave: 116.

At first sight the method leaves enormous gaps in the law, but in fact it is a very economical way of covering a great deal of ground with few examples, since the other alternative, e.g. the natural death of a distrainee who is a son, could theoretically be deduced by simple logic, although in practice knowledge of the common law would be required.

The same scientific method with a double set of variables is in evidence in the goring ox provisions in CH 250-252:-

1) ox gores a head of household *(awīlum)* as it passes along the street - no liability, 2) warned ox gores son *(mār awīlim)* - fixed payment 3) the same gores slave - lower fixed payment.

---

85 For the added complication of the *mār/mārat muškēni m* see the detailed discussion of these paragraphs under *Injury* below.

86 "If a man is owed corn or silver by a man and he takes a distrainee from him and the distrainee dies naturally in the distrainor's house, that case has no claim." We are not informed of the identity of the distrainee; in fact it is likely to be a subordinate member of the household and not its head. This is not, therefore, a perfect example, since the first sequence must yield in part to the logic of the legal institution under discussion. The first member of the first sequence here will be "someone", and it does not matter what his status is, since there is no liability anyway. The following example, on the other hand, provides a more perfect symmetry.

The method of the sequences is the same for distraint and goring ox, but there is a difference in the substantive law. In the middle case, of liability for a son, the goring ox sequence has a fixed payment instead of *talio*. We suggest that this payment represents ransom for the owner's *son's* life, given a price-limit because of the slightly lower level of culpability (there was no initial intention to harm, causation was indirect and as the result of an omission, not an act). The same payment of 1/2 mina, it will be noted, is demanded for unintentionally killing the son of a man in an affray.[87]

We now turn to the provisions of CE. This code applies the same distinction as CH between head of household, son and slave. CE 54-58 discusses the goring ox together with two other cases of non-intentional homicide with indirect causation : the vicious dog and the tumbledown wall, the owner having been warned of the danger in all three cases. Upon this set of variables are imposed the variables of status (head of household (lú), son, slave), but in a different order, and as we shall see, there is a reason for this.[88]

First it discusses the goring ox where the victim is a head of household (54) or a slave (55), imposing penalties of 2/3 of a mina and 15 shekels respectively. The same sequence is then repeated for the vicious dog, with the same penalties (56-57). The son is missing from this sequence: what, then would be the penalty in his case? We might deduce that the payment lay between that for a householder and a slave - e.g. 1/2 a mina - but this does not appear to have been so. In the parallel case of the accidental killing of the son of a man in an affray, the penalty is 2/3 of a mina (CE (Haddad) 47a). The penalty is therefore the same whether the victim is a head of household or a son, and the reason, we suggest, is that in such circumstances only vicarious revenge is permissible, even when the victim is a head of household. The measure of culpability is the same as that of the man who pushes someone into a fire in HL 44a. What the pecuniary penalty of 2/3 of a mina represents, then, is a fixed ransom in lieu of vicarious revenge.

The son, and he alone, appears in the final case of the sequence, CE 58. Where the owner of a wall has been warned that it is dangerous "but he did not strengthen his wall and the wall

---

87 The question may be asked what the payment represents in this sequence when the victim is a slave. It is not likely to be revenge, but rather a system based on replacement of the slave, as in CH 231. CU 21b and CL 12-13 consider the possibility of commuting the replacement into money. In more serious cases double replacement is demanded: CE 23. The small payments in cases of physical injury to a slave may therefore represent a proportion of a slave's value, and qualify as a simple debt. See the discussion of the "jurisdiction" rule of CE 48 below.

88 The sequence opens with a further variable - ox gores ox - which does not concern us here.

collapses and causes the son of a man to die - life *(napištum)*, the king's jurisdiction *(ṣimdat šarrim)*."

The last two words are a set phrase whose meaning is still not settled;[89] our translation in this context is based on the analogy of CE 48, where penalties up to one mina are said to require litigation before the local court, but "a matter of life" *(awāt napištim)* is for the king himself.

In CE 54-57 the penalties are below one mina; we conclude that *napištum*, "life", refers to ransom for homicide set at one mina (or more). In CE 58 head of household and son are again put on a par, but to the opposite effect. The message is that vicarious revenge is insufficient, even where the victim is a son : the head of household must pay the ransom of his own life.[90]

We have explained the goring ox, etc. provisions of CH and CE in terms of the hidden alternative - ransom in CH and revenge in CE - the key issue in both cases being whether vicarious revenge is possible. These hidden alternatives are brought out into the open by our third source, Ex. 21, 28-32, for which the key issue is also vicarious revenge. The text reads:

If an ox gores a man or woman and they die, the ox shall be stoned and its flesh not eaten, but there is no liability on the owner of the ox.

But if the ox is a gorer from times past and his owner has been warned and has not guarded it and it kills a man or woman, the ox shall be stoned and its owner shall be killed. If ransom is laid upon him he shall pay all that is laid upon him as the ransom for his life; the same rule applies to him whether it gored a son or a daughter.

If the ox gored a slave or slave-woman, he shall pay his owner thirty shekels and the ox shall be stoned.

The first case concerns a 'man or woman' and an ox whose owner has not been warned : there is no liability for the owner. The second case concerns the ox of a warned owner, and the sequence is man, woman, son, daughter, slave. So far, it fits neatly into the pattern of the other two codes, but in dealing with the penalties, it is (fortunately for us) considerably more explicit. The penalty is stated in all cases to be death of the owner, i.e. the head of household *or* ransom of *his* life, even if the victim is only a subordinate member of a household. It was already seen by D.H. Müller[91] that this is the point of the law, but it is not, as Greenberg argues, a specific repudiation of vicarious punishment known from

89 A universal definition of the term continues to be elusive: see most recently Kraus *SDIOP* XI 8-14. Our interpretation in this passage follows Goetze (*AASOR* 31, 133-134): "... (and the offence falls under) the jurisdiction of the king". Cf. Kraus, *RA* 73 (1979) p. 61.

90 The term "life" may imply a limit on that ransom: see below.

91 *Die Gesetze Hammurabis*, Vienna 1903, 166-168.

foreign codes such as CH.[92] The principle is the same as we have seen in CE 24 in the matter of distraint; what is made explicit here is the alternative possibility of ransom. The limit on the ransom is the value of the head of household's life, not the life of his son or daughter, etc. Note also that a fixed payment is set in one instance : the case of the slave, as in the other codes.

It is therefore reasonable to conclude that CE 54 and 56 and CH 251, in laying down fixed payments in the same circumstances, are in fact fixing the amount of ransom in lieu of revenge. The initial basis for that ransom is vicarious revenge only, showing that they take a less severe view of culpability for a goring ox than Exodus. On the other hand, in the case of the tumbledown wall, CE 58 adopts the same view as Exodus, rejecting vicarious revenge as the basis for ransom.

c) Miscarriage

The connection between vicarious revenge, ransom and fixed payments can also be seen in another common schools problem: where striking a pregnant woman causes a miscarriage or death of the woman herself. Here the laws all make a distinction according to the status of the pregnant woman: whether she is a wife or a daughter. To modern thinking, the distinction is meaningless, since the same woman will almost always be both at once, but the Ancient Near Eastern family structure lent it a peculiar significance, which expressed itself in law by the different identity of the plaintiff in the two cases.

Where the husband was still living in his father's undivided household his position in law remained that of a subordinate member : he was a 'son'. The wife therefore would enter her father-in-law's house rather than her husband's and take a place below her mother-in-law's, the senior female of the house. Any injury to her would be an injury to the father-in-law's household, for which he, and not the husband, would claim redress.[93] Strictly speaking, one would have expected her to be called the daughter-in-law of a man, but her status in the household was deemed in law to be that of a daughter. Thus Ex.21,9 requires the head of household to treat a slave-girl destined to be married to his son "according to the law of daughters", meaning like a daughter-in-law of free status.[94] It is the mother-in-law alone who would hold the position of 'wife' in

92 "Postulates", p.23.

93 Contra: Driver and Miles, *The Assyrian Laws*, Oxford 1935, 107-108 and Cardascia *Les Lois Assyriennes*, Paris 1969, 136-137, for whom *mārat awīli* refers to social standing and not to legal status.

94 Sometimes the plaintiff will be the wife's own father, if the couple are living with the wife's family, e.g. AL 'A' 33, 36, 38 and the stories of Jacob and Moses.

that household, since she was the wife of the head of the household, and the latter, her husband, would be the plaintiff in a case concerning injury to her. In view of her higher status, it is not unreasonable to expect more severe penalties where the victim is a 'wife' than where she is a 'daughter'.

(i) Abortion of the daughter's foetus is discussed in at least four different laws. YBC 2177 prescribes a payment of ten shekels (or twenty if the assault is aggravated). CH 209 also prescribes ten shekels,[95] as does HL 17, which talks only of a 'woman' (SAL), but which probably may be included in this category by reason of the size of the payment.

In these three laws, then, a very small payment is demanded, which seems to us to indicate that it was not a fixed ransom in lieu of revenge, but represented a simple debt. In a sense this might still be a form of ransom, but for one's freedom rather than to ward off revenge, since non-payment would in the last resort lead to enslavement by the creditor. We have already mentioned the "jursidiction" rule of CE 48. The full text reads: "And for [.....] from 1/3 mina to one mina, they shall cause him to join litigation; but a matter of life is for the king himself." It is to be noted that there is a lower limit to this scale as well as an upper limit. We suspect that the former is the point at which payments (e.g. 10 shekels for a slap in the face: CE 42) ceased to represent ransom for revenge.[96]

While no strict equivalency in prices can be assumed, it is reasonable to suppose that the other codes contained the same distinction.

AL 'A' 21 appears to demand a heavy payment (2 talents 30 mina of lead) plus fifty strokes and a month of royal corvée, but there is no real point of comparison in that code which would give us its relative worth, and we would tend to class this payment also a simple debt, especially since the two additional penalties would seem unsuitable if the payment were in lieu of the offender's or a dependant's life. On the other hand, CL (Civil) iii 2'-6' demands half a mina, which may well have indicated ransom, at least for vicarious revenge. The second part of that law tends to support this view, as we shall see shortly.

(ii) Abortion of a wife's foetus was a more serious matter. AL 'A' 50-51 prescribes three grades of penalty according to whether the circumstances are aggravating or mitigating: (a) death of the offender himself (b) paying a 'life' *(napšāte mullû)* or (c) a fixed payment (2 mina of lead). The first, we would argue, could be commuted by ransom, the meaning of the second will be discussed

95 Or 5 shekels for the daughter of a *muškēnum*.
96 The payment for injury to slaves (55 and 57) is below the limit at 15 shekels. See note 87 above, and the discussion of ransom for a thief's freedom in Chapter Four.

below, and the third is probably a simple debt, if our onclusions as to AL 'A' 21 are correct.

Our hypothesis as to the first case - death or ransom - is borne out by the parallel of Ex. 21,22.[97] There, the person who causes a man's wife to miscarry may pay the ransom demanded of him by the husband. The upper limit on that ransom must be the offender's own life. It is therefore the mirror-image of the Assyrian law.[98] Likewise, Ex 21, 23 goes on to prescribe "paying a life" (ntn npš) in mitigating circumstances.[99]

(iii) Two laws deal with the case where the daughter herself dies as a result. CL (Civil) iii 6'-7' prescribes the death of the offender himself,[100] a very high penalty, which leads us to suspect that the high sum demanded by this same law for the death of the foetus alone was a fixed ransom, just as the present penalty presumes unlimited ransom.

CH 210 and 212 makes a distinction found only in that code (and which will occupy our attention more fully when we discuss personal injury): if the victim was the daughter of an awīlum the offender's daughter is killed, if she was the daughter of a muškē num, he pays half a mina. On the basis of the evidence above, we would argue that here is no fundamental difference between the two types of punishment; rather they represent a sliding scale in which the upper limit to ransom is vicarious revenge confined to the offender's daughter (i.e. not the life of the offender himself) and its lower limit a fixed ransom in lieu of the same revenge.

(iv) The possibility of the wife herself dying is dealt with only in AL 'A' 50(and not in Ex. 21,23),[101] which prescribes a dual penalty : death for the offender (for the wife's death) plus "paying a life" (for the death of the foetus). The former, in our analysis, sets the highest limit on ransom; the latter is a lesser penalty - a technical term which must be explained in the context

---

97 We have studied this pericope in detail elsewhere (See note 1 above) and our conclusions are relied on here and henceforth in this chapter. A summary of those conclusions will be found under *Price-Fixing* below.

98 V.22: "he (the perpetrator) shall surely be punished as the woman's husband shall impose (ransom) upon him..." (On the word *pllym*, see below).

In our earlier study (p. 58) we entertained the possibility that the revenge could be vicarious. We now consider this unlikely in view of the parallel of AL 'A' 50. It is not clear why in v.22 ransom is mentioned rather than revenge, since there is no price-fixing. There is, however, price fixing in the second and principle part of the law, and considerations of symmetry in the discussion (whose main concern was not the level of punishment) may have been dominant.

99 See n.1 above p.67 and under *Price-Fixing* below.

100 nita-bi ì-gaz-e "he shall kill that *male*". Note the use of nita(=zikarum), and not lú "householder". I am grateful to Prof. Jacobsen for drawing my attention to this point.

101 See note 1 above.

of the price-fixing of ransom.

4. Price-Fixing

We have seen in the Assyrian contract ADD 321 that the alternative to the death penalty is the payment of a named slave. This payment is presumably the result of an agreement negotiated by the parties themselves; in a Middle-Babylonian document, BBSt. No 9,[102] a comparable payment is ordered by the court. A death has been caused in obscure circumstances,[103] and the parties join suit in the royal court. The king orders one of the parties to pay the other seven slaves. It cannot be said for certain that this is in lieu of revenge,[104] but if it was, then we have an example of price-fixing by the royal court.

In CE and CH fixed payments are prescribed in certain cases of non-premeditated homicide,[105] as we have seen, but in quantities of silver rather than slaves. A link betwen the two modes of payment is provided by HL, which has a mixed system. In similar cases of non-premeditated homicide[106] HL requires payment of a fixed

---

102 Ed. L.W. King, *Babylonian Boundary-Stones and Memorial-Tablets in the British Museum* (London, 1912) 57-58.

103 The name (or status?) of a key party in line 3 is missing, as is the pronominal suffix in line 5.

104 There appears to have been some difficulty with the payment, but it was eventually received, although one of the slaves handed over was sick (ll. 11-14).

105 Jackson makes the important distinction (*Essays in Jewish and Comparative Legal History*, Leiden 1975, 91-92) between premeditated and intentional homicide. The latter was not regarded as murder. In the case of a fight, there may or may not have been an intention to kill, but it was not planned in advance. In modern terms we would talk of a defence of provocation reducing murder to manslaughter.

106 Jackson's distinction in the above note applies here. Haase (*Bib. Or.* 18(1961) 14-16) distinguishes three categories in HL : (1) pre-meditated murder (5), (2) intentional but not premeditated killing (1,2: *sullanaz* "in a fight"), (3) unintentional killing (3,4: "his hand sins"), with appropriate gradation of penalties.

As *sullanaz* is in the ablative, Friedrich's translation "infolge eines Streites' is perhaps to be preferred. It connects with the idea of provocation raised in the preceding note. This inter- pretation has not been universally accepted, however. Another school sees in the word a factor of *mens rea*: see most recently Cardascia ("Atteintes Corporelles et Droits Cunéiformes", *Studi in Onore di Cesare Sanfilippo* Vol 6 (Milan 1985) 174 n. 23): "par dol", "volontairement". This explanation is contradicted by another law cited to support it: HL 127 "If anyone steals a door *sullanaz*". One cannot steal a door "par dol" because the element of *mens rea* is already in the verb 'steal'. The verb used would have to be a neutral one, such as 'take'. The stealing of the door was presumably provoked by a dispute over the premises to which it was attached. Cardascia further argues that *sullanaz* in HL 1 and 2 cannot mean the same as HL 174: "If men fight and one of them dies, he shall give 1 slave". The verb *zah* is translated "sich prügeln" by Friedrich, and "to strike in hand-to-hand fighting" by Hoffner. (*The Laws of the Hittites* (University Microfilm, Ann Arbor, Ph.D 1963, p.10), which accords with the noun *zahhai* 'battle'. We suggest that 174 does represent a different situation, namely a sport or joust - hence the very light penalty.

number of male or female slaves, according to the sex of the victim. In a later version of the main text, however, payment for the same offences is expressed in quantities of silver.[107] This is not necessarily evidence of a legal reform,[108] since slaves and silver could equally be modes of payment, and not just any slaves could be given, but they presumably had to have a certain value.[109] And in fact payment in silver was known to the older version: in HL 5 the payment demanded for the murder (and robbery) of a Hittite merchant is 100 mina of silver. Haase[110] finds it remarkable that the obviously premeditated murder of a merchant should be punished with such a fine, instead of revenge as in the Telepinus edict. If it is regarded not simply as a fine, but as a fixed ransom, then it becomes comprehensible - the alternative of revenge is still available to the victim's family if it is not paid. Indeed, the enormous sum of 100 mina in itself conveys a message : either that ransom is unacceptable and the robbers, unable to pay, will inevitably suffer death (after duly compensating for the goods stolen) or, that there is a political aspect to robbery and what is being demanded here is payment from some local leader. The political aspects of robbery in the Bible, as noted by Jackson, were mentioned in the previous chapter. In this chapter we have seen from the King of Babylon's letter to the Pharoah that robbers were acting under the orders of local rulers, and in ADD 164[111] a raiding chieftain is held as surety with his family and land, for compensation for 300(!) sheep stolen (apparently from the crown-prince) and the blood-money for a shepherd killed in the raid until one of his entourage should bring the payment fixed by the court.[112] We therefore incline toward the second alternative in this case: tte 100 mina was the ransom demanded for an act with political overtones.[113]

---

107 KBo VI 4, §II. Friedrich: "Paralleltext".

108 We would therefore modify our earlier-expressed view as to KBo VI4 (RB 92 (1985) p. 256). HL does contain evidence of reforms, but the latter text now seems to us a reformulation rather than a reform of the substantive law.

109 As we have seen, in ADD 321 a named slave is demanded, and in BBSt 9 problems arise because one of the slaves was sick.

110 "Zur Tötung eines Kaufmanns nach den Hethitischen Gesetzen" WdO 9 (1977-1978) 217-219.

111 Ed.J.N. Postgate, Fifty Neo-Assyrian Legal Documents, Warminster 1976, 159-60, No 44.

112 Lines 7ff: "Hani with his family and lands has been taken in lieu of the 300 sheep with their fine (and) in lieu of the blood of the shepherds. Whoever seeks him, whether his governor or major-domo or anyone, shall pay 300 sheep with their fine, etc. .....and release Hani."

113 The statement that ransom is unacceptable is found expressed in a different way in the sardiyas laws of HL 37-38, following the interpretation of Jackson, Essays p. 155.

Comparison should also be made with the robbery provisions of CH 22-24. If the robber is caught, he is to be killed *(iddâk)*. If he is not caught, the municipality must pay one mina of silver to the victim's family. It must be assumed that the term *iddâk* here is not an absolute death sentence but revenge with the possibility of ransom,[114] since it would otherwise be preferable for the victim or his family if the robber were *not* caught.

In HL, therefore, the payment of a number of slaves was not, as has been suggested, the expression of an early stage in the conception of punishment where the purpose was to replace manpower lost,[115] but a fixed ransom for the life of the killer (or of a member of his family),[116] which could equally be expressed in pecuniary terms. ADD 164, the Neo-Assyrian document mentioned above concerning a raider who took 300 sheep and killed a shepherd, gives as the penalty for the latter offence (l.5): ús-meš *ša* lú sipa 1-*en* lú 2 gú-un urudu-meš, literally: "the blood of the shepherd, 1 man, 2 talents of copper (is his penalty)". Postgate comments:[117] "...it is difficult to determine how the enumeration should be broken up, especially as Neo-Assyrian can express 'and' by simple parataxis." Accordingly he translates: '1 man (and -?) 2 talents of copper'. In the light of our discussion above, we would suggest that the penalty[118] for the blood of the shepherd is 'one man, namely two talents of copper' i.e. the payment of two talents of copper as the fixed value of a slave.

The money-value given to a slave for these purposes is not a simple question of economics, as the use of the parallel phrase "pay a life" *(napištam mullû)* shows. At Ugarit, in cases not

114 Whether he murdered or only stole goods.

115 Daube, *Studies in Biblical Law*, Cambridge 1947, p.116.

116 Unless the victim is a slave, where the payment may really be replacement of the slave. Cf. CE 23, where an unjustified distrainor who caused the death of another's slave woman must replace her with 2 slaves, but if the victim is a son or wife, CE 24 demands the death penalty. In HL therefore (and elsewhere) seemingly identical payments for different offences may mask penalties of a different nature, the key being the substantive law unexpressed by the text.

The laconic phrase with which many of these laws end, *parnasseia suwaizzi*, has been the subject of an enormous scholarly literature. There is consensus neither as to the literal translation of the phrase nor as to its legal meaning. While it would be possible to choose from the suggested interpretations one or other that suited our interpretation of the law as a whole, we consider this an unprofitable exercise and prefer to leave the question open. For a comprehensive discussion of the phrase, see I. Hoffmann, *op.cit.* note 45 above, 123-144. Note also Cardascia, *op.cit.* note 106 above, p. 176 n. 25.

117 *Op. cit.* note 111 above, p. 160.

118 The question whether it is in lieu of ransom, and if so, of whose life, depends upon the status of the shepherd and the value of the penalty, neither of which is clear. Is the shepherd a slave of the Prince, as the term *ša* lú-*ti* in line 16 would suggest? By the same token, all subjects may be regarded as slaves of the Prince.

involving homicide, *napištum* refers to a slave, who can be used as means of payment. Thus in 17.337 [119] the plaintiff in a law-suit demands the return of his slaves or substitutes and the defendant duly gives in exchange "7 lives, 3 men and 4 women" (l.8ff. 7 *napšā ti* (ZI. MEŠ) *ina libbīšunu* 3 *amīlu* (LU.MEŠ) 4 *sinnišātu* (SAL.MEŠ)...). Likewise in 17.251[120] the parties to an agreement undertake to pay "10 lives" if they break the agreement (ll.14-15 10 *napšāti* (ZI.MEŠ) *umallûnim*).

In the case of murder, however, the expression "pay a person/life" (*amīlam/napištam mullû*) refers to the payment of a fixed value, namely 1 mina. This emerges from a series of treaties concerning the robbery and murder of merchants from one State in the territory of the other contracting State. In 17.230,[121] if the robbers are caught, they must pay "3 times a man" (*amīla* 3-*šu umallâ*) plus three-fold the value of the goods lost; if they are not caught, the merchant's guild must pay "3 times a life" (*napišta* 3-*šu umallâ*) and the goods in *simplum*. 'Man' and 'life' may be taken as synonyms here, as the earlier examples would indicate.

A similar treaty, 17.146,[122] expresses the payment somewhat differently. The guild of merchants must pay "3 mina of silver as the penalty per man" (ll,12-14: *mullû ša išten amīli* 3 ma-na *kaspa .... ušallamūni*) expressed a little further on as "per man, 3 mina of silver the penalty for the blood" (ll. 34-55: *ša išten amīli* 3 ma-na *kaspa mullâ ša dāmi .... umallûni*).

A third document, 17.158,[123] is a law-suit concerning the murder of a foreign merchant. The defendants, apparently pursuant to another treaty like the two above, are condemned to pay 180 shekels (=3 mina) as penalty (*mullû*).

The last two documents suggest that 3 mina was the standard payment at Ugarit for the murder of a merchant. If this is correct, then it is possible to assume that the payment in the first document "3 times a man/life" refers to the same sum. The picture would then emerge of a fixed sum of 1 mina at Ugarit being the notional equivalent of a person for the purposes of payments in homicide cases.[124] The sum would be payable in *simplum* or in multiples

---

119 PRU IV 168-169.
120 PRU IV 236-237.
121 PRU IV 153-154.
122 PRU IV 154-157.
123 PRU IV 169-171.
124 *Contra*: Paul, *Book of the Covenant*, p. 73 n.6: "he shall pay threefold for this life", i.e. the life of the murdered man. But *napišta* is the direct object of *mullû* In AL 'A' 50, where the same phrase occurs together with an indirect object the latter is expressed differently: *kīmu ša libbīša napšāte* umallâ. Paul renders literally (ibid. p. 72): "in place of her fetus, he shall pay a fine for (the loss of) life". But this is far from a
(continued on the next page)

according to the gravity of the case.

The nature of the payment is ransom, as the phrase "penalty for the blood" indicates. There is the same reference to payment for the blood in ADD 164 and ADD 321. Where it is due from the murderer himself, the alternative to non-payment is revenge. Where it is due from the guild of merchants on the other hand, it is presumably a simple debt.

To return to the law codes, in CE there are three terms involving *napištum*: *dīn napištim*, *awāt napištim* and *napištum simpliciter*. The first, "a judgment/law-suit of life", occurs in paragraphs 24 and 26 with the additional provision: "he shall die." These two phrases, we suggest, deal with different matters, the distinction being as follows. *dīn napištim* shows that no vicarious revenge is possible : the distrainor who killed the son of a man (24) or the rapist who deflowered the betrothed daughter of a man (26) is on trial for his own life, even though his offence was against a subordinate member of a household. "he shall die" shows that the only limit to the ransom of his own life is whatever he can achieve by private negotiation with the victim's father.[125] In other cases an external limit can be set on the ransom of his own life: this is *napištum* (58), which we take to be a reference to "pay a life" (*napištam mullû*), i.e. a sum fixed either by treaty (as at Ugarit), or perhaps by royal order, the court or the traditional law in certain cases.[126] The level of the *napištum* is the notional value of a person, rather than the value that the avenger in his discretion sets on the foregoing of his revenge.[127] Hence CE 58 would impose a less severe penalty, giving the offender the choice of paying a ransom fixed by the king (CE 48), than CE 24, which follows the same principle as Ex. 21,29-31.[128]

AL 'A' 50 has the same dual level of ransom for the offender's own life. A person who causes a wife to miscarry must in principle "pay a life". If the foetus is a first-born son, however, or the wife herself dies, "they shall kill the man/striker" (*amīla/māhiṣāna idukkū*). In the latter case the two punishments are cumulative: death for killing the wife and "paying a life" as penalty for her

literal translation, which would be "he shall pay lives for her foetus". (*napšāte* would appear to be a *plurale tantum*: cf. AL 'B' 2).

125 In ARM 8:1, an adoption contract, the parties themselves set death as the penalty for breach and 3 1/3 mina as the ransom therefor. Ll. 30-31: u 3 1/3 ma-na kù-babbar di-*in na-pí-iš-tim i-na-ad-di-in*.

126 It may actually be 1 mina, as at Ugarit, this being the upper limit of lesser payments in CE 48.

127 In a letter, ARM 13:145, 20-22, a person is said to be judged in a *dīn napištim* and to "pay a life". The context is obscure, and the tone of the letter appears to be sarcastic.

128 *awāt napištim* in CE 48 is perhaps a neutral term, indicating that the court must consider ransom of the offender's life, whether by fixed payment or a higher penalty.

foetus *(kīmu ša libbīša)*. It may seem absurd that the offender would have to ransom his life twice - once by negotiation with the husband and again by paying a fixed ransom - but there is a certain logic to it in that two injuries have been caused by the single act. Cumulation of payments to the injured party is a sign that the remedy is intended to be punitive and not merely compensatory.[129]

Finally, we return to the case of miscarriage by a wife in Ex. 21, 22-25. We have dealt with this problem fully in an earlier study; the following is a summary of our conclusions.[130] The circumstances are a fight in the street where a passing pregnant woman is knocked down and suffers a miscarriage. Two situations are considered: 1) where the actual culprit is identifiable; 2) where he is not identifiable. The latter is the meaning of the term *'swn* ; it does not refer to the death of the woman herself.[131]

Where the culprit is identified he has to pay the ransom for his own life that the woman's husband demands. This, as we have seen, is the same high level of responsibility required in AL 'A' 50 where the foetus is a first-born son.[132] The term *pllym* does not add any limitation to the assessment of the ransom or signal the court's intervention ; the word means 'alone' and refers to the sole responsibility among the parties to the affray of the person who actually struck the blow.[133]

Where the culprit is not identifiable *('swn)*, it is the duty of the

129 It should be noted that cumulation was one of the characteristics of an action in delict in Roman Law, if more than one delict was involved in a single act. See F. de Zulueta, *The Institutes of Gaius* Pt.II, Oxford 1953, p.198.

130 See note 1 above.

131 *Ibid.* 56-58. The word *'swn* occurs three times elsewhere in the Bible, all in the Joseph story. After selling Joseph into slavery, his brothers dip his coat in blood and present it to Jacob. According to Daube (*Biblical Law* 3-15) this is in pursuance of the law in Ex 22, 10-12 absolving a shepherd of responsibility for animals devoured by wild beasts, provided he brings a remnant of the animal as evidence.

Jacob is forced to accept the evidence and absolve the brothers of blame but does not really believe it (Gen. 44,28: "The one went away from me - I said 'He is surely torn to pieces' and I have not seen him since".) For this reason Jacob will not let Benjamin accompany his brothers to Egypt: he fears that another *'swn* will happen to Benjamin as happened to Joseph, i.e. a disaster for which nobody can be blamed.

In the Exodus law the same legal situation occurs because the culprit cannot be identified.

132 Except that the law refers directly to ransom, and not to revenge as might be expected. The reason is not altogether clear; if it were to put the choice of paying ransom into the offender's hands, then it could be stultified by the husband demanding an unpayable sum.

133 *Ibid.* 58-61. Our argument here is from context, but is shown to fit all other references to the same root e.g. Dt. 32,30-31: "For their rock is not as our Rock; our enemies are alone".

local authority[134] to compensate the husband, on the lower scale of a fixed sum : "pay a life" *(ntn npš)*, as in AL 'A' 50, CE 58 and the treaties from Ugarit, where this responsibility likewise falls on the local authority when the robbers are not caught. As a local authority is involved, the payment must have been treated as a debt, although nominally the alternative to revenge.

5. Homicide and Penal Theory

The sources of law in the Ancient Near East assume that there is a natural order of retaliation for causing death.

(1) If the killing was premeditated: death of the murderer himself, irrespective of the status of the victim.

(2) If the killing was manslaughter, i.e. unpremeditated or accidental killing: death of a subordinate member of the killer's family.

(3) For manslaughter of a person without civil status (e.g. slave, daughter's foetus): replacement with a slave.

This order is paralleled in terms of the type of ransom payable.

(1) Ransom of the killer's life at the choice and level set by the avenger.

(2) Ransom of the subordinate's life at the choice and level set by the avenger.

(3) Probably a simple debt, with consequences of the order of distraint of property or debt-slavery for non-payment.

The intervention of the courts and central authorities distorts this natural order in two ways. Firstly, the fixing of tariffs for ransom shifts the initial choice of revenge or ransom from the avenger to the offender. Secondly, the gravity of the offence can be indicated by shifting the level of retaliation permitted from direct to vicarious or vice-versa, whether expressly or by implication, by use of the tariff that indicates direct retaliation *(napištum)* or vicarious retaliation (sum below a certain level e.g. 1 mina).

Three examples may be taken from the cases that we have discussed. Firstly, the negligent builder in CH 229 is put on the level of a murderer, the penalty in principle being death, with only the implied possibility of ransom.The only concession made by the law is that where the victim is a subordinate member of the family, vicarious revenge is allowed. This remarkable severity is perhaps the counterpart to the liability of an owner for dangerous buildings. We have seen that the owner of a tumbledown wall in CE 58 is punished far more severely than in the comparable case of a goring ox, and perhaps the provision in Dt. 22,8 imposing blood-

---

134 *Ibid.* 62-66. This interpretation is based on the comparative material from Ugarit and Dt. 21, 1-9, and explains the shift in the subject of the verb ("You (sing.) shall give...")

guilt for failure to build a parapet on the roof of a new house reflects the same policy.[135]

The second example is the goring ox, where a difference of policy can be seen between the Mesopotamian codes and Exodus. The former sets a low-level penalty, allowing ransom in lieu of vicarious revenge, whatever the status of the victim (above a slave), whereas the latter puts liability on a par with murder,[136] again irrespective of the status of the victim (above a slave).

The third example is robbery. As might be expected, CH 22 treats the offence as premeditated murder - which it is - and prescribes death for the offender himself, with only the implied alternative of ransom of his life. Curiously enough, HL 5 for the same offence provides a fixed payment, but of an amount so far beyond normal measure that any protection it might provide from revenge is surely illusory. Even more curious, however, is the fixed payment demanded by the Ugarit treaties, which seems altogether too lenient (although 3 mina was a not inconsiderable sum). Perhaps, as we have suggested, political considerations play a role here. At all events, only CH, for whom the liability of the robber himself is not the main point of the law,[137] seems to reflect the natural order of retaliation that was expressed so forcefully in the King of Babylon's letter to the Pharaoh.

(B) Injury

The principle that injury gives rise to the alternatives of retaliation or composition is stated expressly, not in the Ancient Near Eastern codes, but in the earliest Roman code, the XII Tables:

If he shatters a limb, it shall be *talio*, unless he has made composition with him.[138]

The code goes on to provide penalties of 300 *asses* for breaking a bone (with the hand or fist) if the victim was a free man, 150 *asses* if a slave, and 25 *asses* for "insult" (*iniuria*).[139]

If, as we have already suggested, the Roman code derived from the Ancient Near Eastern tradition, then the similarity of these provisions to those of the Mesopotamian codes is not surprising. To

---

135 The exact liability involved in this verse is not clear. The phrase "bring blood on your house" could refer to pollution of the building or blood-guilt on the family. If it is the latter, then it might indicate vicarious punishment.

136 Assuming ransom to be possible for murder in the Covenant Code. See the final section of this chapter.

137 The main point is the responsibility of the local authority to the victim and his family where the robbers are not caught.

138 SI MEMBRUM RUP(S)IT, NI CUM EO PACIT, TALIO ESTO. Riccobono, *Fontes*, VIII, 2.

139 VIII, 3-4.

be noted firstly is the sequence free man, slave, which is imposed upon the penalties. Then there is the gradation of penalties from retaliation to high fixed payments to a low fixed payment. The latter is for *iniuria*, interpreted by classical jurists to be all *other* injuries,[140] but in classical law *iniuria* was the delict of insult or outrage by words or conduct, including physical injury. The association of injury and insult reveals what *iniuria* originally meant in the XII Tables : a slap in the face. All injury carried an element of insult but a slap was pure insult without the injury. Confirmation from within Roman Law comes from the anecdote of L. Veratius, who at a later period when inflation had destroyed the value of this ancient tariff is said to have amused himself by slapping people in the face and then ordering a slave who followed him with a bag full of money to pay each of them the 25 *asses* fixed by the XII Tables.[141] Confirmation from without comes from the same association of the slap in the face with physical injury that occurs in CH and CE.[142]

In the light of the Near Eastern evidence, we would interpret the gradation of penalties as follows:

1)   For serious injuries - revenge or ransom at the victim's choice. The effect of the talionic principle is to limit revenge to an injury commensurate with that inflicted and indirectly therefore to reduce the amount of ransom-money that can be demanded.

2)   For less serious injuries - a fixed payment, but with the possibility of revenge (presumably limited by *talio*) if the payment is not forthcoming.

3)   For minor injury or insult - a simple debt.

This is the system that we have posited for CE, where a series of injuries is presented like a price-list : biting off nose - 1 mina, an eye - 1 mina, a tooth - 1/2 mina, an ear - 1/2 mina, a slap in the face - 10 shekels, severed finger - 2/3 mina, broken arm - 1/2 mina, broken leg - 1/2 mina, broken collarbone - 1/3 mina, injury (unclear) - 10 shekels.[143] CE 48, as we have seen, requires the parties to join litigation for all [cases(?)][144] from 1/3 mina to 1 mina. In our interpretation this means that all the above injuries are subject to talionic revenge if the fixed payment is not made, except for the slap in the face and the "injury" (probably minor) for which the payment of 10 shekels falls below the minimum and therefore constitutes a simple debt. In spite of appearances therefore, CE did

---

140 Gaius, *Institutes* III 223.

141 See H.F. Jolowicz, *Historical Introduction to the Study of Roman Law*, Cambridge 1952, p.287.

142 As already noted by Müller, *op. cit.* note 91 above, p. 203.

143 CE 42-47 + (Haddad) 47a, which also prescribes 2/3 mina for killing in a fight.

144 A iii 42: about three signs broken.

know the talionic principle.

The incomplete injury provisions of CU in our opinion also reflect the same system. CU 16 demands 1 mina for shattering a limb with a club, CU 17 2/3 mina for a severed nose, and CU 19 apparently 2 shekels for some other injury (unclear)[145] The parameters and gradation are therefore in line with the XII Tables and CE.

The same we would argue is true of HL, which likewise appears to prescribe only money payments for injuries. How the principle worked in practice, however, we cannot say in this case, since it is not possible to correlate the money values with those of Mesopotamia, and the changes recorded within the laws[146] and those in the parallel text present a confusing variety of scales.[147]

Finally, we come to the provisions of CH 196-214. They can be divided into five legal problems, the last two of which - unpremeditated wounding or killing in an affray (206-208) and causing a miscarriage or death thereby (209-214) - have already been dealt with. The principles that we elucidated for the last two problems in the context of homicide apply equally to injury. Let us examine the first three problems in detail.

1) 196: If an *awīlum* puts out the eye of the son of an *awīlum*, they shall put out his eye.

197: If he breaks the bone of an *awīlum* they shall break his bone.

198: If he puts out the eye of a *muškēnum* or breaks the bone of a *muskenum* he shall pay 1 mina of silver.

199: If he puts out the eye of an *awilum's* slave or breaks the bone of an *awī lum's* slave he shall pay half his value.

Two comparable injuries are considered together. The status sequence imposed upon the problem shows four variables instead of three: a head of household *(awīlum)*, a son (dumu *awīli m*), a person of an inferior or poorer class *(muškēnum)*, who is presumably a head of household since elsewhere his son is another variable,[148] and a slave (arad *awīli m)*.[149] Note that the sequence of variables relates to the victims only: the offender is throughout an *awīlum*.

The problem begins with the famous talionic principle, which applies equally whether the victim is a son or head of household. It therefore not only confines the revenge to 'like for like', but

145 CU 18 is too broken for reconstruction; Finkelstein (*JCS* 22 (1960) p.70) restores the injured member in CU 19 as z[ú?-ni?] "his tooth" (iii 1), but this is more than uncertain from the traces, and may not be the correct reading of the sign KA.

146 E.g. para. 7 drastically reduces a payment from 1 mina to 20 shekels.

147 V-XV. Not to mention different criteria for liability: cf. 7 and V.

148 Para. 208.

149 We doubt that the qualification *awīlim* adds much here, but it is possible that the code had in mind a further variable, i.e. a *muškēnum's* slave, if the *muškēnum* were not too poor to own slaves, that is.

excludes the possibility of vicarious revenge. Contrast this with
the boast of Lamech, to have slain a boy for a wound.

The next section treats the eye or bone of a *muškēnum* equally, but
only in terms of a money penalty, albeit a relatively high one. On
our thesis, the contrast is not absolute: the implied alternative to
talionic revenge was ransom, limited by the perceived value of the
offender's eye or bone, while failure to pay the *muškēnum* would
entitle the victim to revenge - within the talionic limits, it must be
presumed. Seen in this way, there is a slight advantage to the
awīlum: where his victim is a *muškēnum* the choice of paying
ransom initially lies with him and is a fixed sum.

We have thus arrived at the crucial question which was the
starting-point of Finkelstein's theory: why does the distinction
between the penalties (albeit formulated differently by us) run
along the lines of *awīlum/muškēnum*? By way of preface, we
should state that we will not attempt to solve "the ever-vexing
problem of the *muškēnum*".[150] Sufficient for our purpose is the
general observation that we agree by and large with Kraus' view[151]
that *awīlum* and *muškēnum* are relative terms. *awīlum* in general
includes *muškēnum*, but in the paragraphs under discussion is
contrasted with it. The distinction is between an upper class and a
lower one, but there is no need to assume a rigid class structure for
which there is no other evidence; the distinction may essentially
be one of wealth.[152]

Let us now look at the problem from the point of view of ransom.
Supposing an *awīlum* a member of the richer classes, puts out the
eye of a *muškēnum*, a member of the poorer classes. If ransom were
allowed, limited only by the talionic principle, i.e. the value that
the *awīlum* placed on saving his eye, it would be an excellent way
for a member of the poorer classes to enrich himself. There is a
conflict between the penal principle, for which harm to the
offender is the most important fact, and the compensation
principle, for which the benefit to the victim is the most
important. The ransom-money system serves both, providing
compensation plus a penal element, and serves them well as long as
the offender and the victim are of relatively equal standing. But
here the victim's eye is not worth anything like as much as the
offender would pay to save his. It is not worth as much objectively
because compensation is not merely for pain and suffering but for
the insult or outrage involved, as we have seen from the Roman
Law, and, regrettable though it may be, the value of one's honour
does depend on one's wealth and standing. The perception of CH

---

150 See Yaron, *Eshnunna*, 83-88 for a summary of the debate.
151 *Vom mesopotamischen Menschen* 92-125, esp. 106-109.
152 Hence the reduction for a *muškēnum* in divorce-money payable: CH 140.

was therefore that in these circumstances ransom had to be curtailed in order to accommodate the compensation principle. If there is any distinction between criminal law and delict in CH, then it lies herein, but the two are not mutually exclusive. The purpose of the code is to find a reasonable balance between the penal and the compensation principle, which continue to exist in a single penalty. It does therefore protect the rich, as Finkelstein concluded, but against unfair profiteering from ransom.[153]

2) 200: If an *awīlum* knocks out the tooth of an *awīlum* who is his equal, they shall knock out his tooth.

201: If he knocks out the tooth of a *muškēnum*, he shall pay 1/3 of a mina of silver.

In this problem the same principles apply. There is one offender, an *awīlum* , and two victims, but further distinctions of social level are introduced, so that the discussion really covers a much wider possible range of victims. Since the objective value of a tooth cannot vary so much, we can again conclude that the element of honour is at issue in deciding the proper level of ransom.

3) 202: If an *awīlum* strikes the cheek of an *awīlum* who is older than he, he shall be struck with 60 strokes of an ox-hide whip in the Assembly.

203: If the son of an *awīlum* strikes the cheek of the son of an *awīlum* who is like him (in age), he shall pay 1 mina of silver.

204: If a *muškēnum* strikes the cheek of a *muškēnum* he shall pay 10 shekels of silver.

205: If an *awīlum* 's slave strikes the cheek of the son of an *awīlum* , they shall cut off his ear.

In this problem the variables have been expanded even further. There are three basic victims, an *awīlum* , a *muškēnum* and a son, but with further gradations between them. We have interpreted those gradations as being of age, but they could be of some system of rank otherwise unknown to us. The major variations are in the offender, of which there are four basic categories: *awīlum, mār awīli m, muškēnum* and slave. This is because the offence is one of pure insult, and the most aggravating factor will be where the offender has a lower status than the victim.

The question that arises is whether the alternative to the payments prescribed (or to ransom) was talionic, i.e. slap for slap? We are inclined to doubt it, since two ends of the social scale are given with much more severe penalties: a public whipping and the loss of an ear. The median may have been a lesser whipping.[154]

---

153 The sentiment that ransom worked unfairly against the rich may be reflected in Prov. 13,8.

154 CE 42 has a much lighter penalty : 10 shekels. Whether it is significant that this is the same penalty that CH prescribes for a *muškēnum* is not clear.

4)   206:   If a man (awīlum) strikes a man (awīlum) in an affray and inflicts a
             wound on him, that man shall swear "I did not strike with malice
             aforethought" and shall pay the doctor.
      207:   If he dies of his blow, he shall swear, and if he (the victim) is the son of
             an awīlum he shall pay 1/2 a mina f silver;
      208:   If he is the son of a muškēnum he shall pay 1/3 of a mina   of
             silver.

The problem of unintential wounding/killing in a fight brings us
full circle to the discussion of homicide. The penalty for wounding
is pure compensation, paying the doctor's fee, and this popular
schools problem may have been used to contrast it with cases where
talio would apply as an alternative. Liability for causing death in
these circumstances has already been discussed; we would only add
that here the distinction between awīlum and muškēnumis purely
in terms of money, and a small amount at that (1/2 mina to 1/3
mina). The distinctions of honour that apply to wounding are less
appropriate to death. Note also the variables of status, which are
much fewer: the offender is an awilum throughout, the victim is a
head of household (awīlum) in the case of wounding and a son in
the case of killing, either of an awīlum or of a muškēnum.
    The subtle distinctions of status introduced by CH give us some
insight into the relationship between the codes and the courts.
Where the parties come before the court in a case of wounding or
death, it would appear that the court has the power in all but
premeditated murder to set a limit on the ransom demandable and
to insist that payment be the first choice. The principles on which
the court sets ransom in the individual case depend firstly upon
general principles of justice, such as the talionic ideal or
mitigation by vicarious punishment, secondly the relative status of
the parties, and thirdly, in some cases at least, the mental
element.[155] The law-codes attempted to express these principles so
as to provide jurisprudential guide-lines, but Babylonian science
was incapable of formulating principles and was forced therefore
to express itself by individual examples. The inevitable result was
price-fixing of ransom, while attempting to make the tariff more
flexible by imposing upon it sequences of variables, such of those of
status. The most sophisticated attempt is that of CH, which adds
to the commonly-used triad head of household, son, slave various
subtler distinctions of status. These increase in proportion to the
element of insult in the offence, since it is here that the court itself
will have to make the subtlest distinctions in fixing the ransom in

---

155 See Cardascia, op. cit. note 106 above. We agree with Cardascia that the laws
on wounding dealt primarily with intentional assaults, unless otherwise stated. But
see our remarks in note 106 above.

the individual case.

Likewise, CH and the other codes, by manipulating in individual examples the application of talionic and vicarious penalties or even the size of a pecuniary penalty, could convey a message as to the principle involved without actually being able to say it in the express terms that modern legal science has available to it.

There is therefore little point in trying to match the tariffs in the codes to penalties found occasionally in recorded law-suits. Of course many of the sums prescribed were hallowed by tradition and mechanically applied, but the court did have to take into account all the circumstances of the case. It looked to the code, not for an exact, mechanical precedent, but for the principle that the code indirectly laid down through its examples.[156]

IV. THE BIBLICAL SYSTEM

The foregoing discussion on homicide and injury in the Ancient Near East has included many contributions from biblical sources - the law on the goring ox, the pregnant woman and the unintentional injury on the one hand; information from the narratives on murder and revenge, on the other. The laws in the Torah on murder and wounding, however, have certain features not found in the cuneiform sources: the right of asylum and the prohibition on ransom. Discussion of these laws has therefore been postponed until now, so that we can examine how these laws with their special features relate to the overall picture from the Ancient Near East.

As far as murder is concerned, we have seen that the law in the biblical narratives fits into that picture without any friction. Premeditated murder gives the right to revenge by the victim's relatives,[157] with the choice of accepting ransom.[158] Possibly the

---

156 Jackson ("Principles and Cases" in *Essays*, 64-74) argues that Babylonian law dealt in cases, not principles. We would argue that it dealt in principles but could only express them as cases. The principles can be extracted, but by applying the *native* cultural and social concepts.

157 2 S. 14, 6-7. According to Phillips ("Another Look at Murder" *JJS* 28 (1977) p. 112: "This (2 Sam.14) has long proved an embarrassment to those who still believe that blood vengeance operated in ancient Israel, that is that the clan which had suffered the death exacted retribution from the clan which had caused it through the agency of the next of kin. But a blood feud can only arise between members of different clans." It is not at all an embarrassment because we do not accept the premise that vengeance was only between clans. Vengeance was not a blood feud but a legal right enforced by the court and subject to its rules. It could apply within the family as much as between families.

158 2 S. 21,3-7. It has been suggested by H. McKeating ("The Development of the
(continued on the next page)

king may act on the family's behalf if they are not able to do so.[159]

In the law codes, murder is first dealt with in Ex. 21,12: "He who strikes a man and he dies shall be killed". Some scholars[160] interpret this rule as excluding composition. There is no explicit statement of course; their argument is based on the peremptory language of the verb: "*must* be killed". M. Buss, on the other hand,[161] translates the verb "he may be *killed*", i.e. that it does not command an execution, while Jackson[162] argues that an underlying right to composition in this and other provisions of the Covenant Code cannot be excluded.

In our opinion, we are as much entitled to assume the implicit alternative of ransom here as in CU(Yildiz) 1, if supporting evidence can be found. We would pray in aid firstly the same evidence that we used to interpret the Sumerian law and secondly the fact that the act in v.12 turns out to have two consequences, one of which is that the offender is not, in fact, killed. If the act was not premeditated he may seek asylum in the local temple (v.13). Presumably he would not stay there for ever, holding on to the altar, but once he had been cleared of premeditated murder[163] could negotiate a ransom with the victim's family[164] or perhaps pay a ransom fixed by the court. Were the victim's relatives then to kill him it would be murder. Were he to be found guilty of premeditated murder, the public authorities[165] would be obliged to hand him over for revenge, as in the Nippur trial.[166]

Law on Homicide in Ancient Israel" *VT* 25 (1975) 59-62) that the Gibeonites, being Canaanites, have a different conception of murder than that of Israel. As far as the legal treatment of murder is concerned, both they and King David to all appearances are applying the same conception as we have seen for the Babylonians, the Egyptians and the Hittites, internally and in international relations. There is no reason *a priori* to assume therefore that either Israel or Canaan have their own separate system; express evidence is required. What the Cannanites do with the bodies afterwards may relate to their own special religious rituals, but it does not affect the legal procedure.

159 Suggested by McKeating, *ibid*, p. 52. Cf. The role of the Babylonian king in his letter to the Pharaoh concerning murdered Babylonian merchants (El-Amarna 8, discussed above).

160 Paul, *Book of the Covenant* 61-62, Phillips, *op.cit.* note 157 above, 108-109; cf. Greenberg, "Postulates", p. 12.

161 "The Distinction between Civil and Criminal Law in Ancient Israel" *Proceedings of the 6th World Congress of Jewish Studies* 1973, Vol. I (1977), p.56.

162 "Reflections on Biblical Criminal Law", *Essays*, 41-46.

163 There was a right to protection for everyone, including premeditated murderers, but only temporarily. See Weinfeld, *op.cit.* note 46 above, p. 73.

164 Or extract an oath from them as in IK 1, 50-53.

165 This is the force of the 2nd person singular "you shall take him" in v.14. See Westbrook, *op. cit.* note 1 above 65-66. In this case it might refer to the temple officials.

166 Where a subordinate member of the family is liable, then it is the head of household's responsibility to hand him over. This would explain the role of the widow in 2 S. 14,7-8.

That the avengers are the other party in all this procedure may be deduced from the fact that the killer flees in the first place. Were his act a public crime to be punished by a public body after examination of the evidence, then asylum would do him no good and would serve no purpose anyway, since a court of law is not a hot-head bent on hasty action. Only if there exists a right of the avengers to take revenge without prior inquiry into mitigating circumstances is asylum necessary.

This interpretation is confirmed by Dt. 19,1-14. There the asylum is a particular city,[167] but otherwise the circumstances are the same: a man has killed another, he reaches asylum, his case is examined and if it was accidental he is not subject to revenge; if it was premeditated, he is. What was only implied in Ex. 21,12-14 is here made explicit : the other party is the redeemer of blood; it is from his hot-headed revenge that the killer flees; it is to him that the condemned murder is handed over by the public authority. We see from the right of asylum that the right to revenge is a shield, not a sword. If used before the circumstances have been clarified it is a defence against further revenge by the original killer's family. Once the matter is in the hands of a court, the avengers must act in accordance with their verdict. If that verdict is premeditated murder, all well and good - the avengers will receive him for execution (or ransom). If the verdict is a lower level of culpability, they must act in accordance with the verdict, e.g. vicarious revenge[168] or a fixed ransom. The laws in Ex. 21,12-14 and Dt. 19,1-14 deal with two opposite extremes; in the intermediate case of death in a fight, for example, it is not to be supposed that the killer got off scot free.

The law in Num. 35,9-34 assumes the existence of the same system. The parties are explicitly stated to be the killer and the redeemer of blood (vv. 12,24). The killer has a right to asylum (v. 12), while the redeemer's right to kill him elsewhere is a defence against further revenge (v.27). If the killer is found guilty of premeditated murder by the court, he is handed over to the redeemer of blood for execution (v. 21). And what we have been forced to infer from the other two sources - the right of the avenger to take ransom-money instead of revenge - is revealed as an

---

167 On the question of the character of the cities of asylum, see most recently Weinfeld, *op. cit.* note 46 above, 72-78. Cities of asylum were not confined to Israel, but were an ancient and widespread phenomenon, albeit not mentioned in the cuneiform law codes. A somewhat different view is expressed by A. Rofé , "The History of the Cities of Refuge in Biblical Law" *Scripta Hierosolymitana* 31 (Jerusalem 1986) 205-239.

168 On this question see Chapter Three.

explicit assumption about the existing law.[169]

But it is at this point that Num. 35 parts company with the other two sources. For it assumes the existence of ransom only to forbid it[170] entirely in the case of premeditated murder (v.31) and for return of the killer from exile in other cases (v.32). Instead, in the latter case exile in the city of asylum is given a time-limit - until the death of the high priest, after which the killer is presumably free of all obligations (v.25).[171]

Before considering the rationale for this difference, we must note a parallel dichotomy between the sources in the case of injury. In Ex. 21,24-25 there is a list of injuries similar to those in the cuneiform codes. In our interpretation, however, as we have mentioned[172], the context is the responsibility of the local authority for injuries to passers-by by persons unknown. They represent fixed sums to be paid by the authority according to the injury, just as the authority must "pay a life" where the injury is the death of a foetus. The question of revenge and ransom is therefore not directly in issue. From the first part of the same law, however, and from the earlier laws on the goring ox, it may be deduced that if individual responsibility were at issue, the whole system of revenge, ransom and fixed payments in lieu of revenge would apply.

In contrast, Lev. 24,17-21, in presenting a similar list of injuries (and death), unambiguously demands retaliation without the possibility of ransom:

> If a man kills any human being, he shall be put to death. One who kills a beast shall make restitution for it : life for life. If anyone maims his fellow, as he has done so shall it be done to him : fracture for fracture, eye for eye, tooth for tooth. The injury he inflicted on another shall be inflicted on him. He who kills a beast shall make restitution for it; but he who kills a human being shall be put to death.

169 The above discussion follows the line of argument presented by S. Loewenstamm in more summary form in "The Laws of Adultery and Murder in Biblical and Mesopotamian Law" *AOAT* 204 (1980) 150-152. Much is made by Finkelstein (*The Goring Ox* 273-274) and Phillips (*op.cit.* note 157 above, 123-126) of the absence of any role for the deceased or his family in Dt. 21,1-9, the ceremony of the heifer. But as Jackson points out, (*Essays* 48-49) this is an argument from silence; there is nothing to exclude the possibility of payment to the family under another rule. Phillips replies (*ibid.*) "... the striking failure of Deut. 21:1-9 to substantiate the view that punishment for murder was a matter for the family...to whom compensation could be paid is none the less remarkable..." It is not at all remarkable if the role of the family was taken for granted.

170 As Jackson (*Essays* p.46) remarks: "A legislator does not waste his energy in condemnation of acts which are not done."

171 We cannot exclude the possibilty that such a time-limit existed in the other sources, but the criterion of the high priest's death bears the special stamp of the Priestly source.

172 Op. cit note 1 above, and see pp.84-85 above.

We have explained[173] this passage as an interpretation of the Exodus formula to show that "pay a life", meaning a fixed sum refers only to animal life; where humans are concerned, paying a life or a limb, etc. means literal retaliation. Like Num. 35, therefore, this passage assumes the existence of ransom and even fixed payments as the alternative to revenge in the common law, and polemicizes against it. The similarity of attitude in the two passages is not surprising, since both derive from the Priestly source. If we add to them the famous verse in Gen. 9,6, also from the Priestly source, requiring that a killer's blood be spilled in retaliation, the picture emerges of a consistent attitude peculiar to this school of thought.[174]

The question is therefore, why were the Priestly circles so adamantly opposed to the universal practice of accepting ransom in lieu of revenge? Their motivation appears to be connected with the Priestly concept of pollution and purity.[175]

In Num. 35,33 there is a reference to pollution of the earth as a result of the killing. The idea that a killing polluted the site of the crime is not confined to the priestly source nor indeed to Israel;[176] what is peculiar to this source is the statement that the pollution cannot be removed by ransom. In the same passage there is a prohibition not only on ransom of the killer's life but, curiously enough, on a ransom agreement whereby the killer can return from exile (v. 32). The correct explanation, in our opinion, is that proffered by P. Segal:[177] the measure is designed to protect the high priest, who is ritually polluted by the presence of a killer in the city. Hence the killer can only return after his death. On this hypothesis, of course, the "high priest" is not, as is usually assumed, the high priest of the whole country or, as Weinfeld argues,[178] of the city of refuge, but the priest of the city where the killing took place.

---

173 *Ibid.*

174 According to McKeating (*op. cit.* note 158 above, p. 65), the effect is "to take the punishment of homicide finally out of the hands of the kin group or local community and to place it firmly in the hands of the priesthood..." But it does not. It is not the priests who act as judges in the city of refuge; the system of revenge by kin is assumed to be *the* system – instead an attempt is made to influence the behaviour of the next of kin.

175 For a systematic exposition of this concept, see T. Frymer-Kensky, "Pollution, Purification and Purgation in Biblical Israel" *Essays in Honor of D.N. Freedman,* Philadelphia 1983, 399-414.

176 Cf. Dt. 22,8 and HL 6. Accordingly it cannot be this element alone which changes homicide into a sacral offence, as McKeating (*ibid*) argues.

177 *Liability under Divine Jurisdiction* (Ll.D. dissertation unpublished – Hebrew University 1986) p. 190 n.lc.

178 Op. cit. note 46 above, 74-75.

There is also a subtle difference in the concept of pollution: the area, and the priest who lives within it, are polluted not merely by the crime (which might be cleansed by ransom or some ritual) but by the continuing presence of the offender. The means to remove this pollution is removal of the offender himself – by execution or banishment.

The cuneiform sources provide no parallel to this conception in respect of murder, but they do in respect of another type of offence. Certain forbidden sexual acts are thought to bring impurity upon the city and its inhabitants.

CH 154 orders banishment for a man who has had intercourse with his daughter – a strange punishment until one realizes that it is designed to remove the impurity from the city. But the most detailed evidence of this attitude comes from the Hittite sources.

HL 187-200 catalogue a series of sexual offences, such as incest, bestiality and the like, the punishment for which is death or banishment. Even where the act is pardoned or is said not to carry punishment, the offender may not approach the king nor ever after become a priest. Hoffner explains[179] that this is to prevent ritual pollution falling upon the king (who is a priest) or the local temple.

In the case of banishment, the Hittite Instructions to the Commander of the Border Guards[180] provide further details and a significant parallel. The town that banishes a person who has committed a defiling sexual act (hurkel)[181] must then ritually purify itself.[182] *No-one may allow the banished offender to return,* under pain of punishment.[183]

It appears, therefore, that the Priestly source in the Bible applied to homicide common conceptions of pollution familiar from other spheres (of which sexual abominations may have been only one), the remedy for which was in terms of execution or banishment and to which ransom was not relevant.[184] In a sense, we have pushed our inquiry a step forward without coming closer to the solution, since the question remains why this application was made.

179"Incest, Sodomy and Bestiality in the Ancient Near East", *Orient and Occident* AOAT 22 (1973) 81-90, esp. p.85.

180 Ed. Einar von Schuler, *Hethitische Dienstanweisungen* AfO Beiheft 10, 1957, 36-59.

181 Equivalent to Hebrew *tbl*: Hoffner, *ibid* p. 90.

182 III A 14.

183 *Ibid.* lines 15-16. The nature of the punishment is not clear.

184 Hoffner (*ibid.* 86-89) claims on the basis of some broken texts that at some point the Hittites replaced banishment with a purification ritual upon the offender himself. We are not certain that this is the correct interpretation, but the present condition of the sources does not allow a more definite interpretation.

Perhaps some help may be gained from the Priestly version of punishment for injury. In Lev. 24,17-21 the term used to describe injury is *mwm* 'blemish'. This is also the technical term for physical defects that render a priest unfit to offer sacrifices in the temple.[185] It is possible, therefore, that these prescriptions had their origins in a code of discipline applying to the priests themselves or to the sacred precincts within their jurisdiction. The rules of homicide may likewise have originated in a much narrower sphere: a concern to keep the area of the temple and its priest free of pollution brought by the entry of a person who had killed.[186]

EXCURSUS - WHY STONE A GORING OX?

Among the guilty of homicide whose fate we have discussed in this chapter, there is one omission : the goring ox. According to Ex. 21,28, the ox that gores a person to death "shall surely be stoned and its flesh shall not be eaten."

These few words have placed a heavy burden upon the unfortunate ox, their rationale being not only the subject of considerable debate among scholars, but also the starting-point for wide-ranging theories as to the nature of biblical law. The discussion has centred on two points : (1) the unusual nature of the ox's execution, not being ordinary slaughter but stoning coupled with a prohibition on eating its flesh; (2) the absence of any reference to the fate of the ox in the parallel laws of CH and CE.

Earlier commentators understood the form of death to indicate that the ox was considered a murderer; it was a sign of a more primitive point of view than the Mesopotamian, where the matter was treated rather as a civil offence.[187]

For Greenberg, the ox is indeed a murderer, but this is not a sign of primitive thinking; on the contrary, it reveals a religious conception which is unique to Israel: "A beast that kills a man destroys the image of God and must give a reckoning for it. Now this is the law of the goring ox in Exodus: it must be stoned to death. The religious evaluation inherent in this law is further evidenced by the prohibition of eating the flesh of the stoned ox.

---

185 Lev. 21,17-21, esp. v. 19.

186 The Hittite Instructions to Temple Officials lay down the death penalty for temple officials who offer sacrifice when ritually unclean. See *ANET* p.209, para. 14. Note Jackson's utilitarian explanation (Essays p. 50) of the priestly ban of ransom: "an attempt by the priestly author to appropriate the proceeds", which also places the rule in the context of the temple administration.

187 Driver and Miles, *The Babylonian Laws,* Vol. I p. 444; H. Cazelles, *Le Code de l'Alliance,* Paris 1946, p.57.

The beast is laden with guilt and is therefore an object of horror."[188]

According to Loewenstamm,[189] it is this religious cast of thought reflected in the legal responsibility of beasts which is foreign to the secular spirit of Mesopotamian law.

Finkelstein[190] shares the view that a difference of values between the biblical and Mesopotamian systems is reflected in the ox's punishment, but disagrees with the definition of the ox's crime as murder. He points out that stoning is never the penalty for someone condemned to death for intentional homicide. The appropriate phrase is "he shall be killed" (*mwt ywmt*) and in Num 35, 19 the actual procedure is described using the verb pg'" to strike (with a weapon)". Finkelstein reviews the use of stoning in the Bible and concludes that it is punishment for crimes that strike at the moral and religious basis of the community as a whole, these crimes being "insurrections against the cosmic order itself". They therefore apply essentially to crimes that can be defined as treason - against God or some lesser master : citizens against the king, sons against fathers, a fornicating daughter against her father, idolatry and blasphemy against God.[191] The ox, therefore, albeit involuntarily, has committed "treason" by killing a human being, who is its superior in the hierarchy of Creation. This also explains why its flesh may not be eaten: it is under the ban (*ḥrm*) like an idolatrous town or the goods of Achan and must therefore be destroyed, not enjoyed.[192]

Finkelstein's analysis is open to a number of criticisms. Firstly, it is not possible to confine stoning to a certain type of crime, namely "treason", however widely defined. For example, in the case of the betrothed girl who fornicates it is not only the girl who is stoned but also the man, for having "violated his neighbour's wife" (Dt. 22,23). There is no way that he can be regarded as on a different hierarchical level than the husband; it is simply an offence against one's neighbour. And if such an act is in some way an offence against the "cosmic order",[193] then there is no reason why every other serious offence, including murder, should not be so regarded, and duly punished with stoning.

Secondly, the prohibition on eating the flesh does not say what is to be done with the carcass of the ox. The *ḥrm* laws, on the other

---

188 "Postulates", p.15. Followed by Paul, *Book of the Covenant* p.79.

189 *IEJ* 7(1957) p. 196.

190 *The Goring Ox*, 26-29.

191 *Ibid.*, p. 28.

192 *Ibid.*

193 This is the only way to explain stoning for gathering sticks on the Sabbath (Num. 15,32-36).

hand, are very specific in this matter : the corpses of the offending persons and their property are to be burnt (Dt. 13,16; Jos. 7,15). It would be pointless to prohibit eating of the ox's flesh if that were the procedure implied to follow its stoning.

Jackson[194] agrees with Finkelstein that stoning is not the appropriate form of execution for homicide, but offers a different rationale for the punishment. Noting that stoning exists not only as a judicial punishment but also occurs in an extra-judicial form, i.e. lynching, he suggests that stoning was primarily a measure of community protection against the goring ox, not of punishing it. This was for the utilitarian purpose of removing the danger of a domestic animal turned wild. Jackson even goes so far as to suggest[195] that the beast was not always stoned *to death*, since this is not explicitly stated, but in the early conditions of a semi-nomadic community, was driven away into the desert. As regards the prohibition on eating its flesh, Jackson explains[196] that this derives from the manner of its passing: the carcass is within the category of *ṭrfh*, animal flesh torn in the field, consumption of which is forbidden by Ex. 22,30.

Both Jackson's alternatives are open to criticism. Phillips[197] points out that the intention behind the stoning must have been to kill the beast, since it is immediately followed by the prohibition on eating it. And if it is to be killed to protect the public, then as Loewenstamm remarks,[198] there is no special rationale for stoning. It could be slaughtered in the ordinary way.

Finally, Van Selms[199] attempts to explain the stoning as a declaratory act by the community to negate the possibility of a blood-feud. Since stoning is action by the whole population, the community is declaring thereby that the ox and no-one else carries the blood-guilt. Everybody who has taken part in the stoning is afterwards a witness in case the relatives of the dead man would try to lay the bloodguilt on the owner of the goring ox.

The difficulty with this view is that, where the owner has been warned of the ox's propensity, he does in fact suffer death in addition to the ox (Ex. 21,29). Van Selms [200] replies that the owner can only ransom himself because the ox will be killed, i.e. the bloodguilt can be put upon another culprit. But ransom is the choice of the victim's relatives, not the owner, and if they choose to exact

194 *Essays* 108-116.
195 *Ibid.*, p. 115.
196 *Ibid.*, p. 116.
197 *JJS* 28(1977) 109.
198 *Encyclopaedia Miqra'it* Vol. 7, Col. 605.
199 "The Goring Ox in Babylonian and Biblical Law", *Ar.Or* 18/4 (1950) 328-330.
200 *Ibid.*, 329-330.

his death, then the ox should theoretically not be killed.[201] V. 29 leaves no doubt, however, that the ox is also killed in this case.

In summary, neither murder, treason, public safety nor shifting of the bloodguilt provides a fully satisfactory explanation for the unusual method of dispatching the goring ox. We therefore wish to suggest a totally different approach to the problem, which combines both utilitarian and religious considerations.

By way of preface to our thesis, some remarks are necessary on the absence of any mention of the ox's fate in the Mesopotamian provisions. The conclusion that nothing was done to the ox is in our opinion unjustified, indeed, the reasoning by which that conclusion has been reached is methodologically unsound. It is a negative argument from silence - that what is not stated did not exist - and nothing could be more inappropriate for the law codes, which never deal with any problem in a comprehensive manner. It is all the more unjustified in this particular case, since it assumes a lack of common sense on the part of Mesopotamian authorities.

An ox which has attacked[202] and killed a man is a public danger and must be disposed of. The point is perhaps better made by referring to an example that is more familiar to the modern reader : the parallel case of the vicious dog in CE. It is not credible that the local ward, which is responsible for such matters,[203] would simply leave a vicious dog that has killed a man to roam the streets at will, or even rely on its master to keep it from doing harm, a task in which he has pointedly failed. The obvious answer would be to see that the dog is destroyed, in this as in any other society. The fact that the point is not discussed in the context of an academic problem on the owner's liability is fortuitous; it is reasonable to assume that such measures were part of the common law.

Like Jackson, therefore, we see the destruction of the ox in the Bible as a purely utilitarian measure. There is no need, in our view, to seek further for explanations based on the guilt or punishment of the unfortunate animal, or to suppose some ideological dichotomy

---

201 Van Selms, *ibid.*, rejects the idea of divided responsibility, which would in any case contradict his basic thesis.

202 As Finkelstein (*The Goring Ox*, p. 24) recognized, this is the key factor, absence of which absolves the owner of liability in paragraph 250: "The decisive circumstance in § 250 is that the accident occurred while the ox was "walking along the street". This is careful and deliberate language. It implies that the ox was "walking along" under proper control by its owner (or whoever was in charge of it), so that the ensuing accident was not the result of negligence on the owner's part. The further implication is unavoidable that the death was due to the victim's own carelessness; he apparently wandered - perhaps absentmindedly - into the animal's path."

203 It issues warnings to the owners of dangerous animals, decrepit walls, is informed of local betrothals (CT 45 86) and acts as the local court of first instance.

between Israel and Mesopotamia. What stands in contradiction to our view is the method of destruction: why not slaughter the ox in the normal way? The answer, we suggest, lies in the history of the religion of Israel.

The centralization of the cult in Jerusalem promulgated by the book of Deuteronomy was accompanied in chapter 12 thereof by the authorization of non-sacrificial slaughter. The reason for this permission has long been recognized:[204] "... before the reform all slaughter - except that of game animals - was deemed to be a sacral act and was prohibited even for non- sacrificial purposes unless the blood was sprinkled upon the altar." The slaughtering of a domestic animal for food was therefore deemed to be an act of sacrifice, and the subsequent meal itself was a part thereof, being a communion meal in which the deity took part.[205]

The Covenant Code, which contains the goring ox provisions, certainly pre-dated the Deuteronomic reforms.[206] Against this background, we see that the authority that orders the owner of a goring ox to destroy it faces a problem. If the owner (or his family) is allowed to slaughter the animal in the normal way, i.e. with a knife, it will be deemed to be a form of sacrifice. Two reasons may be advanced as to why this is objectionable.

Firstly, it may be said that the animal, having killed a human being, is unfit for sacrifice to the deity - it has a moral, if not a physical, blemish. This is certainly a possibility and would go some way to restoring the idea that the ox is attributed with some form of culpability. We prefer, however, a second and to our thinking more straightforward explanation : to allow the owner to sacrifice an animal that has to be slaughtered for reasons of public safety would be to give him an undue benefit. He would be allowed to profit from the fact of having made an offering, which is after all assumed to result in some divine reciprocation.[207] The same applies if he were allowed to eat its flesh: not only would he have the material benefit of the meal, but it might be interpreted as a communion meal with the deity.

One possible solution to the authorities' dilemma would be for someone other than the owner or his family to sacrifice the ox (assuming it to be an acceptable sacrifice). This, however, is not as easy as it may appear. If a third party killed the beast without

---

204 M. Weinfeld, *Deuteronomy and the Deuteronomic School*, Oxford 1972,

205 See V. Maag, "Erwägungen zur Deuteronomischen Kultzentralisation" VT 6(1956) 10-18, and R. de Vaux, *Studies in Old Testament Sacrifice*, Cardiff 1964, 36-37.

206 See Paul, *Book of the Covenant* 43-45 and the literature cited therein.

207 It may be that the owner had in any case to make some sort of expiatory offering. It would be wrong for him to be able to use the animal that must be destroyed in any case in fulfilment of this extra obligation.

giving value to the owner, ownership would not pass[208] and the sacrifice would be considered that of the original owner. If the victim's family killed it they could be said to have received it in payment of the owner's obligation *ex delicto*, but this would be something the law would wish to avoid. If the owner is unwarned he is under no obligation (v.28); there is no reason therefore why the victim's family should profit any more than he. If the owner is warned, his payment is his own life or the ransom thereof ; there is no reason for the ox to be paid in addition and a danger that it might be deemed payment in lieu. A solution in this direction, which is speculative anyway since there is no hint of it in the text, is therefore improbable.

The most obvious course is to adopt a form of slaughter which cannot be identified with sacrifice. This immediately rules out burning, which would be a holocaust-sacrifice. Of the other known ways of killing men or animals, hanging is not a practical solution for an ox. By a process of elimination we arrive at stoning, which is never used as a means of sacrifice.

This, we submit, is the very practical but at the same time religious reason for stoning a goring ox and not eating its flesh.

208 Under the 'Prinzip der notwendigen Entgeltlichkeit'. See Westbrook "Purchase of the Cave of Machpelah" *ILR* 6(1971) 29-34.

CHAPTER THREE: MALTREATMENT OF SLAVES

A. KILLING

Ex. 21,20-21 contains the following law:

When a man strikes his slave, male or female, with a rod and the slave dies under his hand, he shall be punished. But if the slave survives a day or two, he is not to be punished; for the slave is his money. (RSV.)

The RSV, by translating the phrase *nqm ynqm* "he shall be punished", begs the key question of what the master's punishment is to be. The term *nqm* elsewhere means 'revenge',[1] and the JPS translation accordingly renders "he must be avenged". But if so, by whom, and in what measure?[2] Already in the Mekhilta the question was raised whether the death of the master or a pecuniary penalty was meant, the prevailing view being the former, by reason of the express terminology.[3] But the question then remains, why not use the standard expression for the death penalty: *mwt ywmt?*

Cazelles' explanation, that *nqm* refers to revenge by the slave's family,[4] leaves unresolved the distinction between the two punishments. If execution by the State was the norm, it is hard to

---

1 The traditional translation of *nqm* has been attacked by G. Mendenhall (*The Tenth Generation*, Baltimore 1973, 69-104). He claims that the root refers to executive action by a sovereign to rescue his subjects from peril. This leads to a bewildering variety of translations grouped around what appears to us to be two opposing concepts: "defensive vindication" and "punitive vindication". There is no need to enter into a detailed criticism of Mendenhall's analysis, as this has already been provided by W. T. Pitard ("Amarna *ekēmu* and Hebrew nāqam", *Maarav* 3 (1982) 5-25) in refuting Mendenhall's thesis. In particular, Pitard shows that the identification of *nqm* with a verb in the Amarna documents, on which Mendenhall's new interpretation rests, is false.

2 M. Noth (*Exodus*, Engl. transl. O.T. Library, Philadelphia 1959, p. 181) surmises that vengeance was executed for the slave by the 'legal assembly'. He brings no further evidence to support this assertion.

3 "You interpret it to mean by the death of the master. Perhaps this is not so, but it means by making the master pay money? .....R. Akiba says: Here "vengeance" is spoken of, and there "vengeance" is spoken of: "Avenge the children of Israel (Num 31.2). Just as there it means by the sword, so also here it means by the sword." Transl. J.Z. Lauterbach, Philadelphia 1935, Vol III, 60-61.

4 *Le Code de l'Alliance*, p. 54.

see why of all cases the killing of a slave should be subject to a different procedure. If revenge by relatives was the norm, as we have argued in the previous chapter, then it must already be implied in the term *mwt ywmt*, and there would appear to be no rationale for the sudden change in terminology.

According to Greenberg, the reason for the distinction lies in the fact that the slave in question is a foreign slave and therefore has no kin at hand to avenge him. Accordingly, the law, in using this special terminology, is demanding that he "be avenged" by Israelite justice.[5] The idea that a Canaanite (as opposed to a Hebrew) slave is intended in this rule was argued by the Mekhilta,[6] but on the basis of an interpretation of the text that is legalistic rather than historical. The text itself gives no indication of the slave's ethnic affiliation, and we see no reason to assume that it is different from that in any of the other slave-laws of the Book of the Covenant, whether the term *'bry* is appended or not.[7]

The enigma of the term *nqm ynqm* therefore remains; indeed, the most recent study by Van der Ploeg[8] ends on a pessimistic note: "..."he shall be avenged"... implies the shedding of the blood of the master of the slave. But one must admit that this leaves us perplexed. The solution may be found in the supposition that *nāqōm yinnāqēm* is not the original expression ..... The expression is purposely somewhat vague (revenged ... by whom?)..."

Nonetheless, an explanation is at hand, if we turn once again to the parallel provisions of the cuneiform codes. For, contrary to what is generally assumed,[9] this provision of the biblical code does not stand in isolation. In the previous chapter we had occasion to discuss a schools problem treated in CE and CH concerning the killing of a distrainee by the distrainor. The principle that we extrapolated from the different provisions was that death in circumstances where the distraint was unjustified[10] was punishable by the death of the distrainor himself, whatever the status of the distrainee, whereas if the distraint were itself bona fide, the principle of vicarious punishment obtained. Let us now look more closely at the provisions of CH:

---

5 IDB Vol. I, p. 738.

6 *Op. cit.* note 3 above, 56-58.

7 For a summary of the Hebrew/*Habiru* problem, see N.P. Lemche, "The 'Hebrew Slave'", *VT* 25 (1975) 136-144. In any case, at the time of the Covenant Code, a non-Israelite slave might be a native of the country and therefore have local kin to avenge him.

8 J.M.P. Van der Ploeg, "Slavery in the Old Testament" *VT* Suppl. 22 (1971) p. 80.

9 Paul, *Book of the Covenant*, p. 69; Greenberg, *loc. cit.* note 5 above.

10 By reason of the debt having already been paid off. In this we follow the view of B.S. Jackson and T.F. Watkins, "Distraint in the Laws of Eshnunna and Hammurabi" *Studi in Onore di Cesare Sanfilippo* Vol. V (Milan, 1984) 411-419.

115: If a man is owed corn or silver by a man and he takes a distrainee from him and the distrainee dies (naturally) in the distrainor's house, that case has no claim.

116: If the distrainee dies in the distrainor's house through beating or maltreatment, the master of the distrainee shall prove it against his creditor (lit.:"merchant") and:if he was the man's son, they shall kill his son; if he was the man's slave, he shall pay one-third of a mina of silver. He shall also forfeit as much as he gave.

The general situation is that a debtor cannot pay his debt. He may be forced under those circumstances to sell his wife or children into debt-slavery under various arrangements as in CH 117 (or possibly himself), or the creditor may exercise his right to distrain upon members of the debtor's household. In either case the result is slavery. In a classic schools problem, the cuneiform codes deal with the question of the rights and duties of the parties (creditor and debtor) when the creditor kills such a slave. It is set in the context of distraint, which is understandable since it is a situation of sharper confrontation than if the parties had reached a contractual arrangement, but it would apply equally in the latter case.

It seems to us clear that the same problem is being treated in Ex. 21, 20-21. The only difference is in the terminology - the cuneiform law uses 'distrainee' instead of 'slave' - but this is not a difference of substance. There was no separate status of distrainee in Mesopotamian law; the effect of distraint was to make the distrainee the distrainor's slave until such time as he was redeemed by payment of the debt. Moreover, the same system was applied in Israel. In 2 K 4,1-2, the prophet's widow, being destitute, declares: "the creditor has come to take my two children as his slaves". In Neh. 5,5 the impoverished debtors complain: "... we have to put our sons and daughters into slavery; some of our daughters have already been made slaves and we can do nothing, as our fields and vines belong to others". The connection between slavery and debt is also shown in the Covenant Code itself, where Ex. 21,2 provides for the release of a slave after six years "for nothing" i.e. without re-payment of the debt[11] for which he was enslaved.

If the same problem is being treated in CH 116 and Ex 21,20, then it is reasonable to suppose that the same, or a similar, solution is proffered in both cases. In other words, the term *nqm* is used advisedly here as the technical term for vicarious punishment. "He shall be avenged" means that the appropriate member of the creditor's family is liable to be killed by way of revenge: if the victim were a son - his son; if a daughter - his daughter. The text

---

11 The same applies to the slave-girl in v.11.

uses the terms 'slave' (*'bd*) and 'slave-woman' (*'mh*). We know from vv. 7-11 that the latter is a daughter, and it is tempting to assume that a male slave here refers to a son. However, the possibility of self-sale by the head of household cannot be excluded, since the terminology is ambiguous, and we must therefore assume for the sake of caution that the technical term *nqm* embraced the whole principle, i.e. that death of the head of household was appropriately revenged by the death of the creditor, as well as subordinate for subordinate, as we have seen in the case of the negligent builder in CH 229-231.[12] It remains for us to examine whether the interpretation that we have placed upon the term *nqm*, albeit in a narrow legal context, finds reflection in its use elsewhere in the Bible.

For the purposes of our investigation, it is necessary to identify the *object* of the revenge, but the passages in which the term *nqm* is used are notable for the non-specific character of that object. The most frequently mentioned revenge is that of God, but God's revenge is not, with one significant exception that we shall discuss below, visited upon named individuals.

God's revenge by way of *nqm* may be divided into several categories. Firstly, there is revenge upon foreign nations for the harm they have done to Israel, which takes the form of war.[13] On the one hand, it is not possible to expect too much discrimination as to the identity of the victims in war, nor can war be as selective as judicial punishment, but on the other hand, the enemy is personified as an individual and God's action as rightful punishment. It might therefore be argued that no vicarious punishment is involved in the widespread slaughter, merely the punishment of the offender himself, personified as a collectivity. Several texts, however, that emphasize the aspect of divine punishment also stress the necessity for wholesale destruction far beyond the needs of the metaphor of nation as person. In particular Is. 34,5-12, dwells on the destruction of heirs: only various birds of prey will be left to "inherit" the land destroyed by divine revenge.[14]

The second category of divine revenge is again collective and the element of punishment receives even greater prominence. The object is Israel, who is being punished for her sins. The punishment is in the form of wide, but not total, destruction through war,[15] plague, famine and the like.[16] In one instance the objects of the revenge are

---

12 And therefore to entertain the possibility that in the biblical law under discussion, if the debt-slave were the debtor's slave, the penalty would be replacement of a slave.

13 E.g. Dt. 32,43; Is. 63,14; Jer. 46,10; 50,15.28; Ezek. 25, 12.14.15.17; Ps. 149,7.

14 Cf. Jer. 51,36.

15 Jer. 5,9.29; Ezek. 24,8.

16 Lev. 26,25.

more closely defined: In Ezek. 24,6-8, God declares his revenge on Jerusalem, "city of blood", in the form of warfare. The victims of the war, however, will not be at random, nor will they be the totality of the inhabitants: "...your sons and your daughters whom you left behind shall fall by the sword" (v.21).[17] The punishment is therefore exacted upon the culprits not through their own deaths but through the death of their children, whom they are indeed enjoined not to mourn (vv. 22-23).

The third category of divine revenge is visited upon certain classes, if not individuals, within Israel who have been guilty of oppression. This is represented by the prophecy in Is. 1,22-31, which does not, however, describe (except in fanciful simile) the form that this revenge will take and does not therefore add to our discussion.

Turning to revenge by individual mortals, we find firstly that it is the prerogative of human leaders through war no less than of the divine. Needless to say, the objects of the revenge are not defined other than to identify them as the members of some enemy nation.[18]

Where the object of revenge is a smaller group or an individual, however, some interesting details are revealed. Jeremiah asks God to avenge him on his enemies, the men of Anathoth, for stopping him from prophesying with threats of death.[19] He couches his plea like a party to a law-suit seeking from the judge a judgment against his opponent: "O Lord of Hosts, who tries with righteousness, who sees into the heart and the mind, let me see your vengeance upon them, for to you I have committed my law-suit".[20] God announces that he will indeed punish the men of Anathoth. It is not upon the culprits themselves, however, that the blow will fall, but on subordinate members of their families: "... the young men shall die by the sword; their sons and their daughters shall die by famine". (v.22). This is nonetheless considered punishment of the guilty heads of household: "They will have no offspring left, for I will bring evil on the men of Anathoth."[21] In like manner, David invokes God to revenge him on Saul, in terms that suggest the punishment following judgment in a law-suit.[22] And ultimately David does achieve that revenge, if not in accordance with his wishes. The over-zealous soldiers who

---

17 *Ibid.* v. 25.

18 Jos. 10,13; Jud 11,36; I S. 14,24; 18,25.

19 11, 19-21.

20 11,20. Cf. 20,12.

21 The AV. has "there shall be no remnant of them" i.e. of the children. This interpretation is followed by most modern translations, but it presupposes in the Hebrew a word like *mhm* "of, from them", whereas the term used is *lhm* "to them, belonging to them".

22 I S. 24,13.

brought the head of Saul's son to David declare: "Behold the head of Ish-bosheth the son of Saul your enemy, who sought your life; God has avenged my lord the king this day upon Saul and his seed."[23] Ish-bosheth was David's enemy and Saul already dead, yet Ish-bosheth's death is considered revenge not only upon himself but also upon Saul; indeed, primarily upon Saul, who alone is accused of an offence warranting such retribution. David, however, regards Ish-boshet's killing as unjustified (v.11). Whether this is because Saul's offence against David did not justify vicarious revenge on his son is not clear.

A closer parallelism is provided by 2 K 9,7, where Jehu is enjoined to kill all the members of Ahab's household in revenge for the murder of God's *servants* the prophets by Ahab (already deceased), through the agency of his wife, Jezebel.

Finally, we return to divine revenge through warfare, but in this case the metaphor of an individual's revenge upon an individual is pursued more systematically. In Is. 47 Babylon is personified as a woman into whose control another (God) gave his dependants (Israel), but to whom she showed no mercy (vv. 1,6). God therefore announces that he will take revenge *(nqm)* upon her (v.3). The form of the revenge is the killing not of herself, but of her husband and children (v.9).

From the above examples, then, we see that revenge, using the term *nqm*, is exacted not upon the wrongdoer himself but either upon the whole group that he represents or upon selected subordinate members of that group, especially children of the wrongdoer. Indeed, where the text does specify the victim of *nqm*, it is invariably a subordinate.[24] None of these examples, however, is within the framework of a legal system. The protagonists are divine or human leaders exercising executive power or discretion rather than judicial authority. Their revenge acquires the character of a judicial sentence only in the imperfect mirror of metaphor. In its functioning in day-to-day law, the principle of *nqm* needed to be more certain, and therefore must have had more clearly defined limits.

There is no text apart from Ex 21,20 that applies *nqm* in a normal legal context, but there are a number of passages in which its application in extraordinary circumstances provides some indirect evidence.

Firstly, there are two cases that we noted in the previous chapter where *nqm* is used to signify revenge upon the wrongdoer's group, but to a degree that is beyond the bounds of civilized law.

---

23 2 S. 4,8.
24 Except for the husband in Is. 47.9. It would appear possible that in rare cases the head of household was vicariously liable for the acts of his subordinates: Cf. Dt. 24,16.

Lamech boasts of killing a man for a wound and a boy for a blow:[25] in the latter case it is unlikely that the boy[26] was the culprit; rather, he was the object of vicarious punishment. The same must be true of Lamech's "seventy-seven times" revenge, which will fall upon the group to which the offender belongs. But Lamech's action belongs to that of the wicked generation before the flood; the implication is that where the rule of law prevails, revenge *(nqm)*, albeit vicarious, will be within much stricter limits.

When Samson comes to claim his bride, he discovers that his father-in-law has given her to another. He therefore decides to take revenge, but on the Philistines as a group, not on the culprit himself.[27] He declares that his revenge is justified, meaning that it will give no grounds for counter-revenge.[28] When the Philistines see that he has burned their crops, they enquire as to the reason and are told that his bride was given to the best man. They then burn the bride "and her father's house" (i.e. her family (v.6)).[29] The difficulties of interpreting the nature of Samson's subsequent response centre on his declaration in the following verse. RSV translates:

"... If this is what you do, I swear I will be avenged upon you and after that I will quit".

This reflects the view of most commentators that Samon's subsequent action is revenge for what the Philistines did to his bride and father-in-law.[30] But the motivation of both parties is not clear: Samson's connection with the bride and her family is now broken - he has been wronged by them and taken his revenge. The Philistines' action will therefore not affect Samson, nor will Samson have any reason to feel wronged by it. Furthermore, the final phrase "after that I will quit" seems lame and without any real function in the declaration.[31] The correct interpretation of the Philistines' motives was, in our view, given by Abarbanel *(ad loc)*: "They did not wish to take revenge on him, but to assuage him, for

25 Gen. 4,23-24.

26 Hebrew *yld* - a young child.

27 Jud. 15,1-8.

28 This is the force of *nqyty* in v. 3.

29 Some translations have "her and her father" following the main Masoretic text, but as Y. Zakovitch points out *(The Life of Samson*, Jerusalem 1982, p. 131 - in Hebrew), it is preferable to follow those Hebrew MSS (and the Septuagint) which add "house", as this phrase is paralleled in 14,15. Accordingly, the bride's father may not have been included among the victims of the Philistine action.

30 E.g. R. Boling, *Judges.* Anchor Bible, New York 1975, p.254, Zakovitch, *op. cit.* note 29 above, 122, 132-133.

31 JPS sees this difficulty and tries to overcome it by translating: "If that is how you act, I will not rest until I have taken revenge on you". This certainly sounds more logical, but is at the expense of faithfulness to the original.

fear of him and because they understood that Samson had acted lawfully."

As A. Van Selms has pointed out,[32] the bride's father committed a serious wrong in giving the bride to the best man, an act that is forbidden by several of the cuneiform law codes. The Philistines therefore recognize the justice of Samson's cause and seek to put an end to his revenge by executing the wrongdoer's dependants.[33] But Samson is not satisfied; he will not accept the execution of the bride and her family as sufficient revenge. In v.7 (on our interpretation) he replies sarcastically: "If you do as such, shall I for sure be avenged, and thereupon cease?" In other words, if the Philistines thought by their action that they would satisfy him they were wrong; he will only stop when he has completed his revenge as he sees fit.

Samson's revenge is thus upon the group to which the offender belongs, but is in exaggerated measure, being in the realm of warfare rather than of legal punishment. Samson himself appears to regard it as no more than tit for tat (v. 11: ... as they did to me, I did to them), but from the reader's point of view, his act is like that of Lamech.[34]

Several other cases, although they record abnormally high measures of revenge, nonetheless suggest by their stressing of the exceptional circumstances that there is a proper limit on revenge.

In Gen. 4,15, in order to protect Cain's life, God declares that seven-fold revenge will be taken on his killer, which must involve victims among the killer's family. Revenge for homicide in normal circumstances is presumably much lower.[35]

In Esther 8,11 the Jews were allowed by royal decree "to gather and defend their lives, to destroy, to slay, and to annihilate any armed force of any people or province that might attack them, with their children and woman, and to plunder their goods". This is referred to in v. 13 as revenge upon their enemies. Their revenge thus takes the form of war in which wholesale slaughter is allowed, as in the examples of God's revenge with which we opened this discussion. Clearly, this cannot be a normal procedure *within* an organized society, and the special nature of the royal decree permitting such action in explicit detail serves only to underline the point.

The analogy of revenge through warfare brings us to the third example, which shows that even war was governed by rules, to

---

32 "The Best Man and Bride - from Sumer to St. John" *JNES* 9 (1950) 65-75.

33 The wrongdoer is the bride's father, but it is not stated that the Philistines killed him; they burned his daughter (the bride) and his "house" i.e. his family. See note 29 above.

34 Zakovitch (*ibid*, p.122) points out that in this instance Samson is not inspired by the divine spirit, as he is on other occasions.

35 Cf. Ps. 79,10.

which "revenge" *(nqm)* provided a special exception. In Num 31, the Israelites are instructed to wage war against the Midianites and "avenge the Lord of Midian" (v. 3). This special war of God's revenge involves the killing of women and children, but with legalistic distinctions: married women and male children but not virgins (vv. 17-18). Failure of the officers initially to execute these orders leads to a rebuke from Moses (vv. 14-16). Killing non-combatants was therefore not part of normal military practice (although it was bound to occur); the special rules of God's revenge expanded the permissible range of victims to those whom we have seen are typical of *nqm*, but at the same time set a new limit. Revenge in law was not an arbitrary measure.

Finally, we come to texts that illustrate the working of nqm entirely within the legal system. Prov. 6,34 refers to a husband's revenge on the adulterer. It does not say what form that revenge will take, but it does add a useful piece of information: the possibility of ransom in lieu of revenge, as we have argued is the general practice in cases of judicial revenge for homicide or wounding.[36]

Our main source of information is Lev. 19,18:

You shall not take vengeance *(tqm)* or bear any grudge *(ttr)* against the sons of your own people (RSV).

Taking revenge involves doing *ntr* to sons. The RSV translation, followed by many other modern versions, assumes that *ntr* means 'keep' (anger understood) as in Canticles, where it is used in parallelism to *nṣr*.[37] But Driver already in 1931[38] showed that the verb here is derived from a different root, which is cognate to the Akkadian verb *nadāru* "to be angry". Current research in Akkadian shows that *nadāru* means more than a state of mind. It refers to savage slaughter, as performed by wild beasts, armies and robbers.[39]

---

36 The question of ransom for adultery in this verse has been the subject of much debate. Jackson (*Essays*, 60-61) and Loewenstamm (*AOAT* 204, 146-151, 171-172) consider ransom to be a part of the penal system for adultery, while this is denied by Greenberg ("Postulates" 12-13), Paul (*Book of the Covenant* p. 98) and Phillips (*JSOT* 20, 17-18). We follow the view of Jackson and Loewenstamm. In the ANE codes there is evidence that revenge for sexual offences could be vicarious: AL 'A' 55 imposes as punishment on a rapist the sexual abuse of his wife; in the Bible, similar vicarious punishment is imposed on David by God for his adultery with Uriah's wife: 2 S. 12,11-12.

37 1,6; 8,11.12.

38 *Journal of Theological Studies* 32 (1931) 362-363. Driver's interpretation is accepted by the latest edition of Koehler-Baumgartner (p. 656). (Note that their reference is incorrect).

39 CAD Vol. N. Pt. I, 59-61.

ntr in this sense occurs in three passages other than Lev. 19,18, each time describing the actions of God and in parallelism with another verb. In Ps. 103,8-9, God is said to be a merciful ruler who "will not requite *(yryb)* for ever; will not always slaughter *(ytwr)*". The first verb, *ryb*, could mean to bring a law-suit, which is unlikely in this context, and is therefore better interpreted here as cognate to the Akkadian *riabu* "to requite", which is used in the sense of the God "repaying" a person's sin, i.e. imposing the appropriate punishment.[40] In Jer. 3,5 the same motif of punishment limited in time occurs, this time in parallelism with the verb *šmr*, which Driver recognized as the equivalent of Akkadian *šamaru* 'to rage'.[41] The unrepentant Israel says:[42] "Shall he slaughter *(yntr)* for ever, or rage *(yšmr)* for eternity?" The action in question is God's withholding of the rains as punishment for the nation's sins (v. 3). Although this will inevitably cause a certain amount of starvation,[43] Israel remains unrepentant in the expectation that rain will eventually come, i.e. that God, like a merciful father or husband (vv. 1,4) will eventually relent.

The important point for our purposes is that *ntr* describes divine punishment which by its nature (drought) falls upon the collectivity. For the last passage, Nah. 1,2, returns us to the image of God punishing a city by its destruction, and the parallelism is with the subject of our discussion, the verb *nqm*: "God takes revenge *(nqm)* on his adversaries; he slaughters *(ntr)* his enemies."

From these three passages we learn that *ntr* refers to mass killing by God through war or the forces of nature as punishment for collective sin, in the same way as we have seen earlier that *nqm* was used. The specific victims of the action are not described, which is not surprising in view of the non-legal nature of the texts, and indeed was the case in most of the similar references for *nqm*.

Our one legal text, however, where the two terms appear in parallelism, is more specific. We may translate Lev. 18,19 as follows:

"Do not take vicarious revenge; do not slaughter the sons of your people."

Thus interpreted, it is a polemic against the practice of killing the offender's children as punishment of the offender himself. This interpretation is borne out by a parallel passage in Dt 24,16, which uses explicit language instead of the technical legal terminology:

40 In the "Counsels of Wisdom" it is said of one who sneers at the poor: "It is not pleasing to Shamash, who will repay him *(irābšu)* with evil", W.G. Lambert, *Babylonian Wisdom Literature*, Oxford 1960, 100/101, line 60. See also AHw 978b *sub* mng. 2: 'vergelten'.

41 *Ibid*, note 38 above.

42 We follow the RSV in taking this verse to be the statement of Israel, not of God.

43 Among the children only? Cf. Jer. 20,22 and 2 K 6, 28-29.

"Fathers shall not be put to death for sons; sons shall not be put to death for fathers. Every man shall be put to death for his own sin."[44]

The practice of vicarious punishment that these two verses inveigh against (they apply no sanction) is that of the common law as applied in the older Covenant Code. In Ex 21,20 and Lev. 19,18 it is described by use of the term *nqm*. We therefore conclude that while the Covenant Code rejected vicarious revenge in the case of the goring ox, the principle was accepted in the case of the slave killed by his master.

We now turn to the second part of the law, which considers a different set of circumstances:

"But if he (the slave) survives a day or two, he is not to be vicariously avenged; because *(ky)* he/it is his money."

The rationale for this negative ruling is not difficult to explain. Whether one understands it as showing that there was no homicidal intention[45] or that the evidence leaves some doubt as to causation,[46] the gap in time does create a different situation where some relief from the normal penalty, although not inevitable, could be expected. The problem is that the rationale actually provided by the text appears to relate neither to intention nor to causation but to an irrelevant factor: the fact that the slave represents a financial asset to his master.

Traditional interpreters[47] have taken the phrase as an affirmation of the master's basic right to beat his slave, while modern commentators[48] take it to indicate that the master has been sufficiently penalized by the loss of his own possession, and thus he is not subject to any further punishment. Both explanations require a great deal to be implied into the bare words: "he is his money".

Accordingly, we prefer a more literal approach, but not on the basis of the accepted translation. The word translated 'because, for' *(ky)* often means 'but, rather', when following a negation. In Gen. 24,3-4 for example, Abraham says to his servant: "....you will not take a wife for my son from the daughters of the Canaanites, among whom I dwell, but *(ky)* will go to my country and to my kindred...."[49] On this interpretation, the phrase under discussion is not explanatory, but provides a different penalty: "...he shall not

---

44 See note 24 above.
45 Paul, *Book of the Covenant* p. 70.
46 Daube, "Direct and Indirect Causation in Biblical Law" *VT* 11 (1961) p.248.
47 See Paul, *Book of the Covenant* p.70 n.5, for references.
48 E.g. Cazelles, *Code de l'Alliance* p. 54; Noth, *Exodus* note 2 above.
49 Cf. Dt 13,10, Is. 7,8. For further examples of this construction, see Koehler-Baumgartner p. 448 *sub* mng. 3.

be vicariously avenged, but he/it is his money." To understand the legal import of this penalty, we return to our discussion of punishment in the previous chapter, where we saw that revenge had as its hidden alternative ransom.[50] In the present situation if the master/creditor kills his debt-slave, the latter's father or relative has the right to vicarious revenge or ransom negotiable on that basis. If death does not immediately result from the blows, then the father or relative loses his primary right to revenge, but the guilty party still does not escape unpunished. In such a case of reduced culpability we would expect a fixed ransom in lieu of revenge[51] - this, we suggest, is what our enigmatic phrase is referring to: "it (i.e. the revenge) is his money (i.e. the debt)". In other words, forfeiture of the debt owing to him is the penalty, being deemed the fixed payment in lieu of revenge appropriate to the case.

In the parallel case of CH 116, the creditor is also penalized with forfeiture of his debt, but it is not clear whether this applies to both deaths or that of the debtor's slave alone. We incline to the view that it is the former and would reconstruct as follows the legal problem that the cuneiform and biblical codes present in partial (but overlapping) aspects: The death has occurred of a debt-slave while in the service of his creditor.

There are several possibilities.

1. He dies of natural causes. In that case there is no liability on the creditor/master, who may still claim his debt. This is dealt with in CH 115, but not in the biblical law.

2. He died as a direct result of mistreatment. This is dealt with by both codes. The debt-slave's father/master/relative is entitled to vicarious revenge or ransom, the latter not being stated expressly, but fixed by CH 116 in the case of a debtor's slave. CH adds forfeiture of the debt, which is not mentioned in the much more terse biblical formulation.

3. He died apparently of natural causes, but there is evidence linking it to a previous beating. This is a difficult case, dealt with expressly by the biblical law alone, but hinted at in CH 116, where the debtor's right to revenge is stated to depend on his ability to prove the causal connection ("the master of the distrainee shall prove it against his creditor"). In this intermediate situation where the evidence is ambiguous, the biblical law effects a reasonable compromise, precluding revenge but providing a penalty equivalent to a fixed ransom by way of cancellation of the debt.

---

50 And revenge in the form of *nqm* expressly so. See the discussion of Prov. 6,34 above.

51 See the discussion on degrees of culpability in homicide in the previous chapter.

B. WOUNDING

Ex. 21,26 reads:

If a man strikes the eye of his slave, male or female, and destroys it, he shall let his slave go free as the penalty for[52] his eye.

The same rule applies in v. 27 for a tooth.

The penalty for wounding fits logically into the principle of revenge and ransom as we have seen it applied to the killing of a slave. In the case of a free man, the normal penalty would be talionic revenge or ransom in lieu. If he were of low status or a subordinate member of the household, it might well be reduced to a fixed ransom. Since the victim here is a slave, the plaintiff, whether it is the slave himself or the father etc. whose debt was the cause of his enslavement, will not be entitled to more than a fixed ransom, and the law, on the same principle as in v. 21, fixes that ransom at the level of the debt owed. Since the slave in this instance is still alive, the effect of cancelling the debt is to secure his release.

C. SEXUAL ABUSE

Lev. 19,20-22 reads:

If a man lies carnally with a woman who is a slave, betrothed (nḥrpt) to another man and not yet ransomed or given her freedom, an inquiry (bqrt) shall be held. They shall not be put to death, because she was not free; but he shall bring a guilt offering for himself to the Lord, to the door of the tent of meeting, a ram for a guilt offering. And the priest shall make atonement for him with the ram of the guilt offering before the Lord for his sin which he has committed, and the sin which he has committed shall be forgiven him. (RSV).

The traditional interpretation of this law[53] sees the circumstances as follows: A, the slave-girl of B, has been assigned by B to a fiancé C. Another man, D, has intercourse with A. The normal penalty for intercourse with a betrothed woman was death (it being considered tantamount to adultery).[54] The law before us expressly recognizes this fact, but mitigates the punishment

---

52 For the grounds for this translation, see Westbrook, RB 93 (1986) .66 n. 63.

53 See e.g. G. Wenham, The Book of Leviticus (New International Commentary on the Old Testament), Grand Rapids 1979, 269-271. And see now B.J. Schwartz, "A Literary Study of the Slave-Girl Pericope - Leviticus 19:20-22" Scripta Hierosolymitana 31 (Jerusalem 1986) 241-255.

54 Dt. 22, 23-24, cf. Dt. 22,22; Lev. 20,10.

because of the betrothed girl's slave status. The guilty party therefore need only bring a sacrifice to atone for his sin.

The scenario thus presented is a complex one, with the interests of four parties involved. In these circumstances, the lightness of the penalty is all the more surprising. Both the girl's master, B, and her fiancé, C, have suffered as a result of D's offence, yet apparently no attempt is made to compensate either for his loss.

Another unsatisfactory detail is the inquiry that is to be held. It is not at all clear what the subject of the inquiry should be; as Wenham[55] points out, every legal dispute would have involved inquiry, so that the requirement seems vacuous.

The legal problems are compounded by the fact that two key terms in the law are *hapax legomena. nḥrpt* is not the usual term for betrothed, and its etymology is not clear,[56] while the translation of *bqrt* as inquiry, derived from the Septuagint, is not the only candidate: the Vulgata refers to whipping and Nahmanides associates the term with *hpqr* "ownerless", i.e. that the slave-girl gains her freedom as a result of the seduction.[57]

Accordingly, Speiser proposed a new translation of the term *bqrt*, leading to an entirely new interpretation of the law.[58] Speiser noted that the verb *baqārum* in Old Babylonian legal documents designated recovery by the proper owner of his property that was in the possession of another and quoted San Nicolò, who had first analysed the term, as translating it "Schadensersatzpflicht". Speiser accordingly interpreted the biblical *bqrt* as a cognate term indicating an obligation to compensate, and analysed the situation as follows: "A slave girl has been spoken for, but she has not yet been delivered to her designated husband. The price agreed upon remains to be paid, in part or in full. In the meantime another man has slept with her. Since the marriage has not been formalized, this is not a case of adultery. Nevertheless, the girl is no longer a virgin and cannot therefore command the ordinary bride price. A double offense has thus been committed: an impairment of economic values and a sin against morality. Each must be redressed. The moral wrong is to be expiated by means of "the ram of guilt

---

55 *Ibid.*, p. 271.

56 See note 57 below.

57 According to N.M. Bronznick ("Two Unrecognized Cases of *Talḥin*", *Studies in Judaica, Karaitica and Islamica presented to Dr Leon Nemoy*, Bar-Ilan 1982, 39-45), the term has two meanings: investigation and fornication (derived from an Arabic cognate, fjr). Both are implied here as primary and secondary connotation - a rhetorical device called *talḥin*. The phrase means "there shall be an investigation" and "it shall be treated as a case of mere fornication". We find the Arabic cognate unconvincing and the idea of a deliberate ambiguity in a legal text equally so.

58 "Leviticus and the Critics", *Yehezkel Kaufmann Jubilee Volume*, Jerusalem 1960, 33-36.

offering". At the same time, the economic damage must also be repaired. ..."[59]

This interpretation has been followed in a number of modern versions, e.g. Wenham translates[60] "damages must be paid" and the JPS "an indemnity". Loewenstamm,[61] however, has subsequently demonstrated that Speiser's argument is based on a misunderstanding. The Akkadian term *baqāru* never refers to a claim in damages but only to an *actio in rem*, a claim for return of one's property. Speiser mentions both possibilities, but the two types of claim represent in law fundamentally different concepts.[62] Thus Speiser's translation of the Hebrew has no basis in the Akkadian.

We would add two further criticisms of Speiser's theory. Firstly, Speiser also confused the concepts of "claim" and "remedy". *baqāru* means the former only. Although a successful claim by the plaintiff will lead to the appropriate remedy being awarded by the court, they are two separate processes with two different subjects. The plaintiff vindicates, not the court. If the Hebrew term were equivalent to the Akkadian, therefore, it could not refer to the remedy awarded by the court, whether damages or otherwise, but only to the procedural step that will lead, albeit inevitably, to that remedy.

Secondly, Speiser's remarks quoted in full above do not make clear who is to receive the compensation for the loss of the slave-girl's virginity. It would appear that her owner is meant, since it is emphasized that the bride-money has not yet been paid. One wonders where this leaves the contractual relations between the owner and the fiancé. Whether the contract is frustrated or not by the damage done to its object,[63] the fiancé's legitimate expectations have been impaired, so that if compensation is to be paid, it would seem unjust for his interest to be ignored. And if it is ignored, then it is difficult to see why betrothal was mentioned at all, since the girl's economic value is impaired in the same measure whether she happens to be betrothed already or not.

Speiser's theory must therefore be rejected as it stands, and Loewenstamm in fact proposes a return to the traditional translation of "inquiry, investigation". Loewenstamm suggests that the subject of the investigation is the girl's status: whether at the

---

59 *Ibid.*, 35-36.

60 *Op. cit.* note 53 above, p.262.

61 *'bqrt thyh' Shnaton* 4 (1980) 94-97 (in Hebrew).

62 Speiser's reliance on San Nicolò's term "Schadensersatzpflicht" was based on a misunderstanding of the German text. As Loewenstamm points out (*ibid*, p. 95), San Nicolò was referring to a seller's duty to compensate the buyer from whom the real owner has re-claimed his property by a successful *baqrum*-action.

63 Which only impairs its value; it does not render marriage impossible, as the doctrine of frustration would in principle require.

time of the offence she was free or still a slave.[64] This is, after all, the factor that determines whether the crime is capital or not. To the objection that mention of such an investigation is superfluous as it is an essential part of the trial, Loewenstamm replies that an equivalent formula is used in Deuteronomy, albeit as a rhetorical device: the requirement that the court inquire diligently into a matter.[65]

With reference to this last point, we would not place any weight on the Deuteronomic phrase. It is used four times: twice each in two cases where the circumstances justify the express mention of an investigation. The first case is a rumour of apostasy, which requires a special inquisition by the public authorities.[66] The second case is instructions to the judges on trial procedure.[67] On the other hand, it is not found in an ordinary ruling on *substantive* law in any of the biblical or cuneiform codes, nor is it to be expected, since such rulings always assume the facts as proven.[68]

Milgrom[69] likewise rejects Speiser's explanation and translates *bqrt* as "investigation". He does, however, admit the problem of the parties' interests as highlighted by Speiser's thesis, and puts forward the following explanation of why the slave-girl's owner receives no compensation.[70] The case is a very marginal one. A slave-girl is considered a chattel, and her owner should normally have been awarded damages for her defloration, as in all the law codes of the Ancient Near East. Because she is betrothed, however, her master is in effect only her partial owner and therefore not entitled to compensation.

It is not clear to us why partial ownership should entirely deprive the owner of compensation. Logically, he should receive compensation in proportion to his interest in the slave. Of course, it is not entirely necessary for the law to mention the question of compensation if its main interest lies elsewhere. But Milgrom's difficulty with the apparent loose ends left by this law derives in our view more from the multiplicity of parties assumed by the traditional interpretation than from any narrowness of formulation.

---

64 *Op. cit.* note 61 above, p.97.

65 *Ibid.*

66 Dt. 13,12-16; 17,2-7.

67 Dt. 17,8-12; 19,15-21.

68 It is not to be confused with the requirement that a case against someone be *proved*, which is found occasionally in the cuneiform codes. The purpose of this requirement is either to allocate the burden of proof or to impose a lighter penalty where the accusation cannot be proved to the normal standard. See e.g. CH 1, 116; AL 'A' 19, 21.

69 "The Betrothed Slave-Girl, Lev 19,20-22" *ZAW* 89 (1977) 43-50.

70 *Ibid.* 44-45. Milgrom's study is mainly concerned with the problem of the type of sacrifice required, which is outside the bounds of our discussion.

We therefore wish to propose an entirely different interpretation, taking as our starting point the fact that there are two unknown terms in the' law. Our task is made considerably easier by the work of the above-mentioned scholars, in particular Speiser, who pointed the way to the correct solution. Let us therefore begin with the term *bqrt*.

Speiser pointed to the connection between the Hebrew word and the Akkadian *baqru/baqāru*. He mistranslated the latter, and his theory was rightly rejected by Loewenstamm.

But what if we were to take the correct translation of the Akkadian term and apply it to the Hebrew cognate? The phrase *bqrt thyh* would mean "there is an *actio in rem*" i.e. "the owner of the property has the right to claim his property back." In this sense, the phrase has analogues in the cuneiform law codes, albeit in negative form. According to CH 250:

> If an ox as it passes along a street gores a man and causes his death, that case has no claim. *(dīnum šū rugummâm ul īšu)*

The term used here, *rugummûm*, is the general term for claim.[71] In this context it means a claim for compensation, which is the appropriate remedy in the circumstances of the case. What is relevant to our point is not the nature of the potential claim but the fact that the law concerns itself through this impersonal phraseology with the question of whether there is a cause of action at all. In CH 123, where a depositor failed to make a contract of bailment or take witnesses, this phrase is again used to deny him a cause of action.[72]

The final example, CH 115, is the most interesting from our point of view. This paragraph is part of the problem discussed in the first part of this chapter, namely the distrainee who dies while in debt-slavery. Where the distraint is justified and death is by natural causes "that case has no claim". If we invert the circumstances of this case and ask who would have a claim if there were a cause of action, then the answer is revealed, as we have seen, by the following paragraph, CH 116. If the slave dies from blows or maltreatment, it is his father (or original master) who may claim. As in Ex 21,20-21, that claim is for revenge or ransom, or at the very least for release of the debt, and Ex. 21,26-27 shows that where the slave is wounded but not killed, it automatically involves his release from debt-slavery. In the circumstances of Lev 19,20, then, there *is* a claim, but it is a claim *in rem*, i.e. not for

---

71 M. San Nicolò, *Die Schlussklauseln der altbabylonischen Kauf und Tauschverträge*, Munich 1922, 172-174.

72 Strictly speaking, one would suppose that a claim against the bailee would be *in rem*, and therefore described as *baqru*, but the more general term *rugummûm* is nonetheless used, being sufficient for the purposes of negating any claim.

damages but for the return of the slave woman to her owner. To identify the latter, we must elucidate the meaning of the second key phrase: *nḥrpt*.

The universal assumption is that *nḥrpt* refers to some form of betrothal or assignment for marriage. There is, however, no philological evidence, since the term is a hapax in the Bible and no cognates have been identified in the other semitic languages. Most modern scholars refer to the study of Z. Ben-Haim,[73] which relies on two rather weak pieces of evidence: the Ethiopic translations of the relevant passages and a statement in the Talmud that in Judah a betrothed woman is called *ḥrwph*.[74] It is possible that the Talmudic account represents an old tradition, but Talmudic marriage law is very different from biblical, and the term may be derived from a late interpretation of the text under discussion. Interpretation of the term *nḥrpt* in our text was already uncertain in early post-biblical times: the Septuagint translates "reserved".

The question remains, if it does mean betrothed, why the normal biblical verb *'rś* was not used. Ben-Haim's explanation is that it was misunderstood in the Talmud; it means betrothed only by promise, i.e. before the payment of the bride-money *(mhr)*, which is a necessary condition for full betrothal.[75] Speiser's analysis above appears to adopt the same view in assuming that the bride-money has not yet been paid in full.

This explanation is unsatisfactory, since this stage of betrothal in itself is sufficient to negate adultery: there is no death penalty for a stranger who has intercourse with a girl who is only promised. On this hypothesis, the reason given by Lev. 19,10 for the absence of the death penalty - that the slave-girl has not yet been freed - would be otiose. We therefore consider ourselves justified in looking in a different direction for the meaning of *nḥrpt*.

We have seen in the earlier part of this chapter that slavery is ultimately connected with debt, which in turn plays an important role in the punishment for abuse of the slave. We would therefore connect the root *ḥrp* with the root *'rb*, 'to pledge'.[76] and translate: 'a slave-woman who is *pledged*'. Such a derivation presents no linguistic problem, since the letters *ḥet* and *ayin* are known to interchange, as are *peh* and *bet*.[77]

---

73 *Leshonenu* 7 (5696) 362-366.

74 T. B. Qiddushin 70a.

75 Cf. 2 S. 3,14 and see Westbrook, *Old Babylonian Marriage Law* AfO Beiheft 23 (forthcoming) Chapter Two.

76 Koehler-Baumgartner, 829-830 *sub* I.

77 We are indebted for this point to the work of Dr. B. Lifschitz, who in an unpublished study on the root *'rb* seeks to show its identity with *'rp, ḥlp* and, incidentally *ḥrp*. We disagree, however, as to his conclusions on the semantic
(continued on next page)

The difficulty that this approach presents is that the element of adultery, necessary to the law, seems to have disappeared. We suggest that it remains, but is to be found in another word in the opening phrase - the Hebrew 'šh, translated 'woman' by the RSV: 'If a man lies carnally with a woman'. The word 'šh in Hebrew is ambiguous: it can mean a female in general or a wife, as in Gen. 30,4 'and she gave him Bilha her slave *as a wife*' (l'šh). In the context of betrothal, the laws refer to the fiancée as a girl (n'rh).[78] As we have seen in Chapter Two, a woman's status in law is that of a wife or a daughter. An 'šh belongs in the former category; a n'rh in the latter. Note especially the law in Dt. 22, 13-21 concerning the newly-wed girl whose husband claims she did not come to him a virgin. In relation to her husband she is always called an 'šh, but in relation to her father the same girl is invariably called a n'rh. We therefore propose to translate the term 'šh as 'wife' here, as in the cognate Akkadian term *aššatu*.

In the result, we have in the protasis a wife who is pledged as a slave. This is a situation well-known from the cuneiform laws. According to CH 117:

If a man is seized for a debt and sells his wife, his son or his daughter, or gives (them) in debt-slavery (*ana kiššātim*),[79] they shall do work in the house of their purchaser or pledgee (*kāšišišunu*) for three years; in the fourth year their release shall be established.

In our law, therefore, a man has been forced to pledge his wife as a slave for his debt, the verb *ḥrp* being a technical term for a particular type of pledge-contract, and while in slavery she has been sexually abused. As to the identity of the culprit, the most likely candidate is, as in the cases of killing and wounding, the creditor, her present master. And the text can be seen to say as much expressly, simply by altering the vocalization of the opening phrase: "If a man has intercourse with a wife, she being a slave pledged to *the* man...(*lā-'īyš*)", i.e. that very man.

We are now in a position to explain the penalties. A creditor has had intercourse with another man's wife, but escapes the normal penalty for adultery because she is his debt-slave. As an owner, he has the right to enjoy the services of his slaves, which would normally include their sexual services. In this particular case,

---

connection: he follows Ben-Haim's interpretation of *ḥrp* as betrothed, and suggests that the connection with 'rb is that both involved promise and obligation. But legal terms must be more exact than this.

78 Dt. 22,23-29.

79 The precise legal nature of the transaction known as *kiššātum* is unclear. It involves selling oneself or members of one's family into slavery, and presumably refers to the particular conditions for release/satisfaction of the debt. See F.R. Kraus, *Königliche Verfügungen in altbabylonischer Zeit, SDIOAP XI*, Leiden 1984, 266- 277.

however, it is an abuse of his power and a breach of the contract of pledge, this not being the purpose of this particular debt-slavery. The creditor's act therefore does not remain without consequences. It is punished in two ways.

Firstly the husband can claim back his wife, that is to say, cancel the pledge (and with it the debt). That is the role of the action *in rem: bqrt*. Secondly, the creditor's act is still regarded as a sin, hence his duty to make an offering in expiation thereof.

The effect of the slave-woman's freedom is not to make the creditor an adulteror where he was not one before; in both cases his offence is adultery. It is rather a question of remedies. If the wife is still a slave, then all the husband can do is to claim back his property. If, on the other hand, she were already redeemed or freed when the act of intercourse took place, then the husband could claim from the creditor the normal penalty for adultery with a free woman - death.[80]

Consequently, there are only three parties: the husband, the wife and the creditor. The rights of the husband fit into the pattern that we have seen for the rights of a father when his son, given as a debt-slave, is abused by the owner/creditor. We would translate the law in Lev. 19,20-22 as follows:

> If a man has sexual intercourse with a married woman, she being a slave pledged to the man and not redeemed or given her freedom, an action lies for her return. They may not be put to death because she was not freed. He shall bring his guilt-offering, etc.

As a postcript to this interpretation we wish to consider briefly the implications for the scholarly debate on the nature of adultery in biblical law. There are two schools of thought:[81] the first, represented principally by Greenberg, Paul, and Phillips, considers adultery to be a crime, an offence against the social order for which the death penalty is mandatory irrespective of the wishes of the husband. The second, represented principally by Loewenstamm and Jackson, sees adultery as essentially an offence against the husband, who may choose to prosecute or may pardon (or accept ransom). The latter school also sees adultery as a sin, but this aspect is punished by a divine rather than a human, tribunal.[82]

If our interpretation of the law in Lev. 19,20-22 is correct, then the legal consequences of adultery, where the wife is still a slave, are expressed solely in terms of her husband's right to bring an action against the adulterer. In the alternative mentioned in the

---

80 The free woman would also suffer this penalty, of course, as an adulteress, unless it was a case of rape. As a slave, on the other hand, she is presumed to have been under compulsion.

81 For references, see note 36 above.

82 Loewenstamm, *op. cit.* note 36 above, 147-148.

law of the wife being free at the time of the adultery, the most reasonable assumption - and the one that we have adopted in our translation - is that it is likewise the husband's rights that are in issue, this time to demand the death penalty. Adultery would therefore be an offence against the husband, as the second school of thought claims. Nonetheless, it remains at the same time a sin against God, as evidenced by the requirement of a guilt-offering.

CHAPTER FOUR:
THEFT AND RECEIVING STOLEN GOODS

Ex. 21,37-22,3 contain the following provisions on theft[1]

[37]When a man steals an ox or a sheep, and slaughters it or sells it, he shall pay five oxen for the ox, and four sheep for the sheep. [1]If the thief is seized while tunneling, and he is beaten to death, there is no bloodguilt in his case. [2]If the sun has risen on him, there is bloodguilt in that case. He must make restitution; if he lacks the means, he shall be sold for his theft. [3]But if what he stole - whether ox or ass or sheep - is found alive in his possession, he shall pay double. (JPS).

The text raises two interrelated problems that we wish to discuss in this chapter. Firstly, why are two different penalties imposed - four-or five-fold in v.37, but only two-fold in v.3? Secondly, the apparently incoherent order of the provisions, whereby the rule as to restitution and insolvency, which should logically follow immediately upon the penalties imposed on the thief, instead is attached to a discussion of the householder's liability for killing the thief.

The distinction between the two levels of penalty has been seen by some interpreters as reflecting the more serious nature of the crime where the extra step of slaughtering or selling the stolen animal has been taken. Thus Rabbi Akiba considered that such a thief had become "established in his sin",[2] while for Noth the thief thereby displays a "systematic evil intent".[3] Such attempts at rationalization have been dismissed by Jackson[4] with the apt comment that the thief who has not yet sold or slaughtered the stolen animal is morally no less blameworthy; he is merely less successful.

---

[1] Following the verse and chapter arrangement of the Masoretic text. In the Vulgate and translations following it (e.g. AV, RSV) the same passage is numbered 22, 1-4.

[2] Tos. B.Q. 7.2.

[3] *Exodus*, p. 183.

[4] *Theft*, p. 133.

A far more promising approach is that of Daube, who ventures an historical explanation.[5] He points out that the passage contains three rules which are not in their logical order : (a) the thief who slaughters and sells, (b) the right to kill a thief breaking in (c) the thief who has not yet slaughtered or sold. The logical order would have been for (c) to precede (b).

Drawing on an analogy from Roman Law, Daube suggests that the reason why the most logical sequence was not followed is that originally the statute contained two provisions: (a) and (b), while (c) is a later amendment. It was, however, appended and not inserted, as logic would require, because the statute was too well-known in its traditional order.[6]

The later provision was added as the result of a development in the law of evidence. The original law contained a crude, objective evidence test: theft was not proved until the stolen thing had been used. Later, a more sophisticated test developed whereby the subjective intentions of the thief were considered. If it could be ascertained that he had the appropriate *mens rea*, then possession alone would be sufficient to establish theft.[7]

Jackson accepts Daube's theory, but qualifies it as regards the stages of development.[8] According to Jackson, even at the earliest stage, sale and slaughter could not have been the only possible evidence for theft. Firstly, he points to the right of the householder to kill a thief caught *in flagranti*. Daube conceded as much, but distinguished between an excusable act in the heat of the moment and the calm proceedings of the court, where the stricter test would again prevail.[9] But Jackson notes that there is a third possibility - that the householder, having caught the thief *in flagranti*, does not kill him but brings him before the court. It is not reasonable to suppose that the householder would then have no remedy, because of the absence of sale or slaughter.[10]

Secondly, there is the treatment of theft in the patriarchal narratives (assuming them to be early). In the account of Rachel's theft of Laban's household gods and of the "theft" of a goblet by Joseph's brothers, possession is assumed to be conclusive evidence of theft.[11]

Thirdly, Jackson considers unfounded Daube's rationale for a strict test in early law, namely the severity of the punishment for

[5] *Biblical Law*, 89-99.

[6] *Ibid.*, 89, cf. 74-77.

[7] *Ibid.*, 90-91.

[8] *Theft*, 42-48.

[9] *Biblical Law*, p. 92.

[10] *Theft*, p. 43.

[11] *Ibid.*, p.44.

theft. He points out that the four- or five-fold penalty is not especially severe, and that there is no evidence that originally the penalty for simple theft was death, as Daube infers.[12] Accordingly, Jackson suggests that even at the first stage use of the stolen property is not to be taken as excluding other methods of proof; it is merely the most common. The test of possession therefore already existed, if in lesser measure, when the law in Exodus was first drafted.

The effect of Jackson's qualifications to Daube's theory is to undermine it altogether. If both tests existed alongside each other at the early stage, there can be no question of an historical development. Nor is there any reason why the law-code should not have included both,[13] or possession alone, for that matter, since it marks the minimal evidence necessary. Jackson suggests that the sale or slaughter test would be more common, and therefore more likely to find expression in the laws, but we see no grounds for this supposition. The sale or slaughter test is less decisive than the possession test, since the stolen thing is no longer directly connected with the thief, having been consumed or passed to other hands and possibly disappeared completely. Indeed, it requires more sophisticated proof, the evidence being necessarily of a circumstantial nature.

Furthermore, as Jackson himself notes, the possession test is already to be found in the cuneiform codes alongside the sale test, at least.[14] The hypothesis of historical development is therefore inherently unlikely; a better approach is to examine the treatment of theft in the cuneiform codes.

The ancient Near Eastern legal tradition contains a classic schools problem on theft. The solution differed from system to system, but the problem remained essentially the same. Let us begin with the exposition in CH 9:

> If a man whose property is lost seizes his missing property in the hands of a man (and) the man in whose hands the lost property is seized says: "A seller sold it to me; I bought it in front of witnesses", while the owner of the lost property says, "I shall bring witnesses who know my lost property:"- the buyer shall bring the seller who sold it to him and the witnesses in whose presence he bought it, while the seller shall bring the witnesses who know his lost property. The judges shall examine their case. The witnesses in whose presence the purchase was made and the witnesses who know the lost property shall declare their knowledge before the god. The seller is a thief; he shall be put to death. The owner of the lost property shall take his lost property. The buyer shall take the money he paid from the estate of the seller.

---

[12] *Ibid.*, p.48. While not agreeing with Daube, we shall argue in part against this last assumption of Jackson below.

[13] Jackson (*ibid.* 132-133) recognizes some of the difficulties arising from his qualifications to Daube's theory, without resolving them.

[14] *Ibid.*, pp. 42-45. See below.

The problem presented is not merely one of theft, but of theft combined with sale, and the resultant conflict between the original owner and the innocent purchaser. The principle that it lays down is of considerable importance, namely that in this conflict between two innocent parties, the loss must fall on the purchaser.[15] For the neat solution proposed by this paragraph reveals its academic origins: in real life the seller, if he is also the thief, will have disappeared or have spent the proceeds and not be worth suing.

In another aspect this law is not only academic; it is apparently in conflict with the common law, as evidenced by contemporary documents and by other paragraphs of CH itself.[16] The penalty for simple theft is stated to be death, whereas the system in practice appears to follow the lines of CH 8 and 265, which demand ten-fold damages for simple theft from an ordinary citizen. Moreover, in the continuation of the problem in 9 itself, in paragraph 12,[17] we find the following rule:

> If the seller has died, the buyer may take five-fold the claim of that very case from the estate of the seller.

This rule makes no sense at all if predicated upon the penalty in paragraph 9 where the seller is executed anyway and the buyer is entitled to simple compensation from his assets. Its explanation lies in a combination of the principle there revealed of the buyer's strict liability (tempered by his right to recover what he can of his loss from the seller) with the normal penalty for theft, i.e. multiple damages. In paragraph 12 the innocent purchaser is being allowed to recoup, at least in part, the payment of multiple damages which he himself has had to make to the owner. "That very case is the one in which the owner has succeeded in exacting from the purchaser not only restitution of the goods but also multiple damages. Thus the multiple damages system applies in principle to the purchaser, albeit innocent, of stolen goods as much

[15] The same attitude is reflected in Roman Law, in which the innocent purchaser can never acquire title to stolen property, even by usucapion. Modern legal ystems, on the other hand, are tending more and more to prefer the purchaser over the claims of the original owner, in the interests of free commerce. See e.g. for the United States: Anderson on the Uniform Commercial Code, 2-403 and the commentary thereto (2nd ed., Vol. 2, 1971).

[16] This question was examined in detail in: R. Westbrook and C. Wilcke, "The Liability of an Innocent Purchaser of Stolen Goods in Early Mesopotamian Law" AfO 25 (1974-1977) 111-121. As will be seen below, this chapter offers a new analysis of some of the problems raised in that article, and reaches somewhat different conclusions.

[17] Paragraphs 10 and 11 deal with two theoretical alternatives to 9: if the buyer cannot produce his witnesses, he is put to death; if the seller cannot produce his witnesses, he is put to death. A fragment of the same problem is represented by CE 40, which is parallel to CH 10.

as to the actual thief. The purchaser can then recover this payment from the seller/thief no less than the price paid for the goods that he has forfeited. Paragraph 12 presents us with this system at work, but deals with a further complication. The innocent purchaser has had to pay multiple damages to the owner, but at a rate (five-fold) lower than that imposed on a thief (ten-fold). He now seeks to recoup this sum from the seller (whether the latter is the thief himself or part of a chain of buyers leading to the thief does not affect the principle) only to discover that the seller has died in the interim. He can nonetheless recover his payment from the seller's estate, a right which still leaves him with the risk of the latter's insolvency.[18]

In summary, theft is presented as a three-cornered affair, involving the owner, the thief who is also the seller, and the receiver of the stolen goods from him. The law applied is that the latter is strictly liable to the owner for multiple damages, but may recover the same amount from the seller.

The three-cornered presentation of theft is continued in the Assyrian Laws, Tablet A, paragraphs 3-6. It is all the more noticeable, since these paragraphs are concerned not with theft in the abstract but with the position of a married woman, and the circumstances are in consequence somewhat special. Paragraphs 3-4 concern the case of a woman who steals from her husband and passes the stolen goods to a receiver. The laws consider the liability of both wife and receiver;[19] indeed a certain linkage is established between their punishment. Paragraph 5 considers the

---

[18] In our earlier analysis of the problem (note 16 above, p.113), we assumed that the innocent purchaser was liable for the same multiple damages as a thief (ten-fold) and in paragraph 12 was being allowed to recoup only half (five-fold), this sharing the burden with the seller's innocent heirs. This is still a possibility, but we now suspect that it might be too "modern" in its legal reasoning. The present suggestion has the merit of being simpler and, as we shall see, in direct parallel to the relevant provisions in other codes.

The basic right of an innocent purchaser to recoup from the seller the penalty paid by him to the owner is confirmed by contempory documents of practice, *ibid.*, 114-117.

[19] Para. 3: If a man is sick or dead and his wife steals something from his house and gives it to a man or a woman or any third party, they shall put to death the wife and the receiver. If a married woman whose husband is well steals from her husband's house and gives it to a man or a woman or any third party, the man shall charge his wife and impose a punishment on her; the receiver who received the stolen property from the man's wife shall restore it and they shall impose upon the receiver the same penalty as the husband imposed on his wife. Para. 4: If a slave or slave woman receives something from a married woman, they shall cut off the nose and ears of the slave or slave-woman, and they shall restore the stolen property in full. The husband shall cut off his wife's nose, but if he pardons his wife and does not cut off her nose, they shall not cut off those of the slave or slave woman, nor shall they restore in full the stolen property.

case of a wife who steals from another man.[20] Here there is no mention of any passing of the goods, but the paragraph is nonetheless shown to be but one side of the coin by that following, which considers the strict liability for theft of a mere depositee from the wife.[21] The three- cornered pattern remains in the draftsman's mind even when dealing with individual aspects of theft or receiving.

The three-cornered pattern is less evident in the Hittite Laws, but it nonetheless plays a key role in the relevant provisions, which must be considered in detail.

HL 57-71 deal with theft of animals and related offences and may be divided into several categories:-

1. Ordinary theft. This is characterized by the phrase "if someone steals...". There are three levels of penalty, depending purely on the type of animal stolen. The somewhat complex provisions as to type of animal may schematized as follows.

Paragraphs 57-59 deal with the most valuable animals, the examples given being a bull, a stallion and a ram. The penalty is fifteen-fold restitution.

Paragraphs 63-65 deal with less valuable animals: a plow-ox, a cart-horse, a goat, and certain species of sheep. The penalty here is ten-fold restitution.

Paragraphs 67-69 deal with a cow, a mare and certain other species of sheep. The penalty is six-fold restitution.

2. The fraudulent finder. Here a different act is described: "If someone finds a .... and "cleans" it (i.e. removes the marks of ownership)[22] and its owner identifies[23] it...."

Paragraphs 60-62 mention a bull, a stallion, and a ram, i.e. animals in the first category of theft, and impose a penalty of seven-fold restitution, which is approximately half of that for stealing the same animals. Although the finder committed a fraudulent act designed permanently to deprive the owner of his property, he did not actively take away the property, and this is

---

[20] If a married woman has stolen something from another man's house exceeding 5 mina of lead in value, the owner of the stolen goods shall swear: "I did not let her have possession of it" and "(There has been) a theft from my house." If her husband agrees, he shall restore the stolen goods and redeem her, and cut off her ears. If the husband does not agree to redeem her, the owner of the stolen goods shall take her and cut off her nose.

[21] Para. 6: If a married woman makes an outside deposit, the receiver shall be liable for the stolen goods.

[22] Following J. Friedrich's explanation (Die Hethitischen Gesetze, Leiden 1959, p.39 n.1). H. Hoffner's suggestion (The Laws of the Hittites, Ph.D. diss. 1963, University Microfilms, Ann Arbor, 59-60), "castrates", is unconvincing. Why would the finder of an animal want to castrate it?

[23] Verb: kanes 'ausfindig machen'. Friedrich, ibid. p.124.

apparently regarded as a mitigating circumstance. Note that the owner here has succeeded in proving that the animal is his and that the ownership marks were removed by the present possessor.

3. The negligent finder. This category is represented by paragraph 71, which begins "If someone finds a horse, a donkey, an ass..."[24] His duty is to report it to the authorities, in which case "if its owner finds it he may rightfully (sakuwassar) take it but he may not seize him as a thief."

The owner's proprietary right is therefore established, but a right to multiple damages is denied. On the other hand, if the finder does not inform the authorities, the text declares him to be a thief. The text does not say what the consequences are of being a thief in these circumstances, but this and other significant details are provided by a later version of the same paragraph.[25] There the finder must have the find witnessed or else will be considered a thief if the owner finds it. His penalty in that case is three-fold restitution. This version adds to the list of lost property an ox, a sheep and even utensils ($\acute{u}$-nu-te ^{meš}), which shows that the list is meant to indicate any lost property: the size of the penalty does not depend on the nature of the property as in ordinary theft or fraudulent finding. As this is the only one of the paragraphs under discussion to be found in the later version it is impossible to say whether the lower penalty reflects a general trend or mitigation by reason of the offence being one of omission rather than active dishonesty. The latter seems to us more likely, in view of the express distinction made in the Laws between degrees of culpability.[26]

4. Innocent possession. Paragraph 66 concerns various types of animal, large and small, which wander over to another herd. The owner of the herd is entirely innocent and accordingly "if its owner finds it he may rightfully take it but he may not seize him as a thief."

5. Paragraph 70 reads:

If someone steals an ox or a horse or a mule or an ass (and) its owner identifies (kanes) it, he may rightfully take it. In addition he shall give two-fold....

All the translations of this paragraph add in brackets 'the thief' as the person who is to make the two-fold restitution. But this cannot be so. The penalty for theft is much higher : six-, ten-, or fifteen- fold. It might be argued that different animals are

---

[24] Added in a variant version: Friedrich, *ibid.* p. 40 n. 22.

[25] KBo VI 4, para. XXXV.

[26] On the other hand, if the fraudulent finder of 60-61 were to pay half the multiple damages payable by a thief for the least valuable category of animals, it would amount to three-fold damages.

involved, but it will be noted that the list is the same as in the following paragraph, concerning the negligent finder, where we have noted that the content of the list is of secondary importance. Nor is there the reduction in the size of the penalty ("...formerly they gave 30...now he shall give 15...") that appears in all the paragraphs on ordinary theft.[27]

Closer analysis of paragraph 70 reveals that it has this special characteristic: it combines the phraseology of the theft paragraphs with that of the finder/possessor paragraphs. From the former it has "if someone steals" and the multiple restitution provision. On the other hand, "if its owner identifies it" comes from the realm of the fraudulent finder, not the thief, while the statement "he may rightfully take it" is altogether out of place in theft, where there could be no doubt as to the owner's right vis-à-vis the thief. The phrase is only found in cases of innocent possession, where the dispute is rather as to ownership between two innocent parties than as to culpability for theft or fraud.

The solution is that the unidentified person who has to pay two-fold is not the thief, but the innocent receiver of stolen goods. The thief stole them, removed their identifying marks and sold them to an innocent purchaser. The owner nonetheless manages to identify them as his property, and is therefore entitled to their return, even though their present possessor can equally prove innocent acquisition. In addition, the latter must pay multiple damages.

The principle is therefore the same as in CH. The innocent purchaser is strictly liable to the owner for the penalty for theft, and must re-coup his loss from the seller/thief as best he can. As in CH, the multiple damages paid by the innocent purchaser are lower than those payable by the original thief - his innocence is admitted as a mitigating factor. The possibility of his recouping this payment from the seller/thief is not mentioned, but in our view was also part of this law.

On this analysis, the two provisions of the Exodus law present no difficulty. In Ex. 21,37, where the thief has slaughtered or sold the animal, he faces multiple damages according to the type of animal, as in HL 57-59, 63-65 and 67-69. The point of the slaughter or sale is to show that the original thief is meant: the animal is no longer in his possession, and his crime has been proved by circumstantial evidence, such as the testimony of the buyer, as in CH 9.

In Ex. 22,3 it is not the same original thief who is the subject but the innocent possessor, as in HL 70. He is not specifically identified, but then neither is he in HL 70, and failure to identify

---

[27] The difficulties were already seen by H. Güterbock, *JCS* 15(1961) p. 74, who took them to indicate that the Hittite Laws were a collection of heterogeneous material.

the subject, or even a change of subject, is a particularly common feature of the ancient Near Eastern codes.[28] Note also that Ex. 22,3, shares two other features with HL 70: there is a longer list of animals than in the law on original theft, formulated in such a way as to indicate that the type of animal is unimportant since the penalty is uniform; and the penalty itself is a lower level of multiple damages than for original theft. As in the Hittite Laws, the possibility of recouping the payment from the seller/thief is omitted, but in our view was part of the law.

We would apply the same analysis to explain the kidnapping provision in Ex. 21,16. RSV translates: "Whoever steals a man, whether he sells him or is found in possession of him, shall be put to death", and, as far as we have been able to ascertain, this is the interpretation universally adopted by translations into modern languages. But it is not what the Hebrew text says. A literal translation would be: "He that steals a man and sells him and he is found in his hand shall be put to death".

It is clear why the literal translation has been universally rejected: as Daube points out,[29] the kidnapped man cannot be sold by the thief and be found in his hand at the same time. But the difficulty disappears once one realizes that the terse Hebrew formulation contains a change of subject:

"He that steals a man and sells him and he in whose possession he is found shall be put to death."

A parallel from CH is instructive here; although it does not deal with kidnapping, it is a valid analogy, since it is concerned with a form of aggravated theft which like kidnapping bears the death penalty - CH 6 reads:

If a man steals property of a god or of the palace, that man shall be put to death and he who received the stolen property into his possession shall be put to death.[30]

The same principle as in Ex. 21,16 is formulated in more express terms, as is to be expected, since the style of CH is in general far more explicit than codes such as CE and the Covenant Code, which tend to a more terse formulation.[31]

---

[28] See Yaron, *Eshnunna*, 58-59.

[29] *Biblical Law*, p. 95.

[30] Cf. AL 'A' 3 (note 19 above), where the same principle applies. The wife who steals from her husband and the receiver of the stolen goods are both put to death.

[31] See Yaron, *Eshnunna* and cf. J. Muffs, *Studies in the Aramaic Legal Papyri from Elephantine SDIOAP* 8, Leiden 1969, 22-23.

We now turn to the second problem mentioned at the beginning of this chapter - the internal order of the verses. The difficulty is succinctly described by Daube:[32] "We would expect the law to speak first about what a thief who has killed or sold the animal has to pay, next about a thief who cannot pay, and finally about self-help, slaying a burglar", whereas the present order is, damages from a thief, self-help, and a thief who cannot pay.

Accordingly, many scholars assume that the order of the Masoretic text has at some point become confused,[33] and translations such as RSV and NEB rearrange the verses in the same order as considered logical by Daube. Even the JPS translation quoted by us, which follows the Masoretic text, considers the self-help provision to be out of place, noting that the person who must make restitution in 22,2 is the thief of 21,37.

Daube himself argues that it is another example of his view of the development of the law, which at first contained only the provisions about payment and self-help, the insolvency provision being tacked on at a later date.[34] There is even less rationale in this case for such a development, since the question of insolvency must already have been at issue in the earliest law.

Jackson[35] argues that the thief who breaks in and the thief of 22,1 are one and the same, the offence being one of theft from a sheepfold.[36] Therefore, having stated that the owner has no right to kill the thief in the daytime, "it is not a large jump in thought to state next the penalty the thief must suffer assuming that the owner does abide by this restriction. ... Thus the verse proceeds 'he (the thief) shall surely pay.'"[37] This phrase therefore refers back to the penalties already mentioned.[38]

The difficulty with Jackson's view is that the penalties of 21,37 are inapplicable to the thief caught tunneling. Since he is obviously on his way in and not on his way out, he will not yet have stolen any animals that could be used as the basis for multiple restitution.

In our view, 22,1-2 describe a different offence to those of the two surrounding verses, and the penalty in 22,2 is linked to the question of insolvency in the same verse. Moreover, all three offences form a coherent whole, which follows a logical order. To understand that

---

[32] *Biblical Law*, p. 93.

[33] E.g. Paul, *Book of the Covenant*, p. 85; Noth, *Exodus* p. 183.

[34] *Ibid.*, note 32 above.

[35] *Theft*, p. 155.

[36] But theft from a house and theft from a sheepfold were treated in the same way: *ibid.*

[37] *Ibid.*

[38] *Ibid.*, p. 51.

logic we must return to our discussion of the basic system of revenge and ransom in Chapter Two.

We have seen that the penalties of death or injury for the concomitant offences in fact express the right of the injured parties to revenge, and carry the implied alternative of ransom. The same principle applied to the penalties prescribed in the codes for theft.

There is no express statement in the cuneiform codes of the revenge aspect of the penalties, as there is for death and wounding, but on the other hand the multiple damages are private actions[39] which go far beyond the bounds of ordinary compensation.

According to CH 8:

If a man steals an ox or a sheep or an ass or a pig or a boat, if it belongs to a god or to the palace he shall restore thirty-fold; if it belongs to a subject he shall restore ten-fold. If the thief has not the means to pay, he shall be put to death.

From this paragraph we can see that the multiple damages are in fact a fixed ransom in lieu of revenge, which itself is set at the death of the perpetrator. Interpreting the provision in this way helps to explain the paradox of CH prescribing the death penalty for theft alongside multiple damages.

In its purest form, the penalty for theft is the right of the victim to kill the thief who stole from him in revenge, with the alternative right to accept from the thief a ransom for his life. Due to the intervention of the law to limit revenge or fix the ransom, the penalty in its purest form is likely to be found in practice only for aggravated theft, just as it is restricted in homicide to premeditated murder. Let us now review the relevant paragraphs of CH, to see if this assumption is valid.

In CH 6, quoted above, the aggravating factor is clear: the stolen property belongs to a temple or palace. Commentators have found difficulty in distinguishing between this provision and CH 8, where the victim is the same.[40] We now consider the difference to be one of *mens rea*. The formulation of paragraph 8 differs from that of 6 in two ways: firstly, the identity of the owner is mentioned only in parenthesis and secondly, the stolen items are of a type that move of their own volition (or at least with the tide) and may thus be found at some distance from the owner's land. The thief, on taking them, would not know to whom they belong, and

---

[39] The initiator of the action is the owner of the stolen goods, as CH 9-11 shows; it is he who receives the multiple damages and is liable to severe punishment for a false accusation.

[40] See Driver and Miles, *The Babylonian Laws*, p.81, who consider 6 to deal with theft from the precincts of the temple or palace, while 8 concerns movable property kept outside, and therefore not *sacra*. In our earlier article, we surmised that they were derived from two separate and conflicting systems: *op. cit.* note 16 above, pp. 113, 119.

cannot therefore be said to have had at the time of taking the intention to steal divine or royal property.

CH 7 reads:

> If a man buys silver, gold, a slave, a slave-woman, an ox, a sheep, an ass or anything else from the son of a man or the slave of a man without witnesses or contract, or receives (it) for safekeeping, that man is a thief - he shall be put to death.

The aggravating factor here becomes clear if we compare AL 'A' 3. There a wife who steals from her sick or dead husband suffers the death penalty, but so does anyone who received the stolen property from her.[41] The circumstances referred to in CH 7 are not, therefore, an innocent, if negligent, omission of formalities.[42] Theft by a subordinate member of the family from the head of household also constitutes a serious breach of trust, and anyone who knowingly (as the absence of witnesses proves) abets the disloyal servant risks an aggravated penalty.

CH 14 imposes the death penalty for kidnapping the son of a man - an obvious case of aggravated theft, with a direct parallel in Ex. 21,16. A more interesting parallel is HL 19, which imposes a payment of six slaves for the kidnapping of a free man. This is remarkably high, since we have seen that the highest payment for homicide in HL is four slaves. It is, however, understandable if the alternative is death. The demand of ransom fixed so high in order to avoid death is a clear message to the initiated as to the seriousness with which kidnapping is viewed.

CH 21 reads:

> If a man breaks into a house, they shall put him to death and hang him up in front of the breach.

Here again, the aggravated nature of the offence is evident. As we shall see, it seems somewhat harsh when compared with the case of the burglar in Ex. 22,1-2, which distinguishes between breaking in by day or by night, but in fact it may not be the same type of offence. From the grouping of this paragraph with those on robbery and looting, rather than with the earlier theft provisions, it would seem to be regarded as a crime of violence rather than stealth, and therefore to constitute a danger to life and limb by day as well as by night.

---

[41] For the text of the law, see note 19 above. If the husband is well, paragraph 4 gives him a discretion as to the punishment of his wife, which must then apply automatically to the receiver. We see no reason why that discretion should not have included death. The husband's illness could not have been an aggravating factor, since the receiver would not necessarily have known of it.

[42] Which is what distinguishes this case from CH 122-123, where the negligent depositor is left without a remedy.

Thus far the paradox has been resolved in a fairly straightforward manner. The crucial provisions of CH 9-11, however, can in no way be fitted into the category of aggravated theft. The explanation for the death penalty here, we consider, lies in quite the opposite direction. We previously noted that these paragraphs are highly academic: they constitute a purely theoretical discussion aimed at establishing the principle of liability among the respective parties. Although framed as if they were an actual case, they are in fact the nearest Babylonian science can come to a discussion of first principles. Consequently, the form of penalty used is the purest form - death at the victim's option - which would certainly apply in theory. The draughtsman was well aware, however, that in practice the intervention of the law barred the victim's option in all but aggravated cases, and consequently saw no contradiction in returning to the system of fixed ransom when discussing practical applications of the principle in paragraphs 12 and 13.

In the Bible, the death penalty is imposed, as we have seen, for aggravated theft in the form of kidnapping. Another example of aggravated theft is Rachel's theft of Laban's household gods.[43] In Gen. 31,32, Jacob, having been accused by Laban of the theft, invites him to conduct a search, saying:

"Any one with whom you find your gods shall not live. In the presence of our kinsmen recognize what I have that is yours, and take it."

Jackson[44] has suggested that the aggravating factor here is the holy nature of the property stolen. This is possible, but we prefer Daube's explanation - that it lay in the search.[45] Daube points to the parallel with early Roman law, where theft was considered aggravated (furtum manifestum) and subject to higher penalties when the thief was caught in flagranti or in analogous circumstances. Such analogous circumstances included hot pursuit and discovery of the stolen goods after a formal search of the suspected thief's premises. There is much stress laid on Jacob's invitation to Laban to search in front of witnesses and "recognize" i.e. formally identify his property.[46] By accepting a formal search, Jacob allowed the theft to take on an aggravated

[43] For the other case in Genesis, the "theft" of Joseph's cup by his brothers, see the excursus to this chapter.

[44] Theft, 165-166.

[45] Biblical Law, 201-207.

[46] Ibid., p. 206.

character[47] (being confident, of course, that nothing would be found) which would allow Laban to exact the maximum revenge.[48]

In the case of ordinary theft, however, the same restrictions applied as in the cuneiform systems. Accordingly, the four-and five-fold restitution in Ex. 21,37 represents, in our view, a fixed ransom in lieu of the death of the thief. As this is not a case of aggravated theft, the ransom demandable is limited and the option is the thief's not the victim's; only if he cannot or will not pay could the victim exercise his right to revenge.

The second offence in the Exodus law, the burglary in 22,1-2, is also connected with a traditional problem in the cuneiform law-codes.

CL 9 reads:

> If a man enters the orchard of a man and is seized there for stealing, he shall pay 10 shekels of silver.

The same theme with regard to a house is discussed in HL 93:

> If they seize a free man beforehand, when he has not yet entered the house, he shall pay 12 shekels of silver...

It is not stated that the purpose of the attempted entry was burglary, but this is clear from the surrounding paragraphs of the code, which all concern theft offences. Furthermore, CE 12-13 shows that there is no legal difference between house and orchard; they are both regarded as examples of the same offence:

> A man who is seized among the sheaves in the field of a subject[49] in broad daylight shall pay 10 shekels of silver. One who is seized among the sheaves at night shall die; he shall not live.
>
> A man who is seized in the house of a subject in the house in broad daylight shall pay 10 shekels of silver. One who is caught in the house at night shall die; he shall not live.

---

[47] According to Phillips (*Ancient Israel's Criminal Law*, p. 141 n. 68): "The fact that Jacob orders the death of the person with whom Laban's household gods are found discloses the absolute power of the head of the clan in patriarchal times, but says nothing about any special category of theft". Jacob undoubtedly has the power to punish his subordinates, but still he must do so in accordance with customary law. A patriarch could no more impose arbitrary penalties than could a king.

[48] Daube (*ibid.* p. 207) argues that the use of the phrase "shall not live" in v. 32 instead of the expected "shall be put to death" means that the culprit is to be handed over to divine vengeance, not to Laban. The idea that the two phrases reflect two different types of punishment is no longer tenable in the light of CE 12-13: "He shall die; he shall not live."

[49] As opposed to the field of the king or of a temple. Our interpretation of the difficult term *muškēnum* here follows Yaron, *Eshnunna* 83-88.

Yaron has shown firstly that the "he shall die; he shall not live" formula refers to self-help.[50] The proprietor is entitled to kill the intruder on the spot without need for legal process. In this the Eshnunna law reveals itself as the closest parallel to the biblical provision,[51] although all the laws mentioned so far are part of the same problem. Thus in spite of the absence of any mention of theft in the Eshnunna text, we can be sure that this was the background to the offence. Yaron's second point[52] is that all the above cuneiform sources deal with a situation where actual theft has not yet been committed. Consequently, the penalty consists of a fixed sum, not related to the value of anything stolen.

We would add that the sums imposed are very low, indicating that attempted burglary was not considered as serious as the completed offence, even though the thief was caught in the act. Indeed, they are so low that it is unlikely that they are in lieu of death.[53] The 10 shekels of CE 12-13 is below the lower limit for wounding in CE 48 (20 shekels) and even less than the penalty for causing the death of a slave in CE 55,57. In lieu of what, then, are these fixed payments? The answer is provided by the biblical law.

Ex. 22,2 states that the attempted burglar "shall surely pay" (šlm yšlm), but does not say what he shall pay. It cannot be related to the stolen goods, since there are none, and JPS' rendering "he must make restitution" is therefore incorrect.[54] What he has to pay is revealed by the continuation of the verse: "if he lacks the means, he shall be sold for his theft".

In our view, the sum that he has to pay is indeterminate because it is the ransom for his freedom, to be negotiated between himself and the victim of his attempted burglary. The person to whom he is to be sold is that same victim himself, in debt-slavery. Falk has suggested[55] that the verb mkr 'to sell' should be rendered 'handed over', i.e. to the victim. While this strengthens our case, we prefer not to rely on Falk's translation, for which he does not adduce

---

[50] Ibid. p. 173.

[51] Where the proprietor who kills the thief at night as a measure of self-help is not liable to revenge, because in the circumstances the burglar "has no blood" to be avenged. See J. Schoneveld, "Le Sang du Cambrioleur - Ex. 22:1-2", Symbolae de Liagre Böhl, Leiden 1973, 335-340.

[52] Ibid., p.181.

[53] Except in CH 21, discussed above. The death penalty there may reflect a difference in attitude, but the gap is so wide that in our view it is more likely that a different offence was intended. We have already pointed out that the law is placed in the context of crimes of violence rather than of offences against property, in contrast to HL 93. The penalty could be a measure of self-help, although there is no distinction between day and night.

[54] Unless one assumes that the verses are in the wrong, or simply an illogical, order. See above.

[55] "Hebrew Legal Terms II", JSS 12 (1967) 241-244.

systematic philological evidence. Likewise we would reject Jackson's translation,[56] following the same line of argument: "he shall be handed over in exchange for the stolen animal". Jackson's translation of *bgnbtw* as 'for the stolen animal' is based on the argument that *gnbh* elsewhere in the Bible means the concrete object of the theft[57] and that the conceptual sense of 'the theft' is too sophisticated for the period of the Covenant Code. But the Covenant Code is no less sophisticated than CE or CL, if not CH, and the same term in Akkadian, *šurqu*, can mean either 'theft' or 'the stolen object', according to context, from the very earliest sources.[58] In any case, if we are correct in taking the penalty as relating to the attempted burglar, then there is no stolen animal for which he can be handed over.

Nonetheless, we agree with the insight of these two scholars that the burglar is being consigned to enslavement with the victim here, while we do not think it is stretching the language too far to say that he is being sold to the victim, with his theft as the price - that being equally the price of his redemption from slavery.

If our analysis of Ex. 22, 1-2 is correct, then the sums payable in the parallel provisions of CL 9 and CE 12-13 represent fixed ransom in lieu of slavery, following the tendency of those codes to set tariffs for ransom.

The final case in the Exodus law is that of the innocent possessor, who must pay two-fold damages. Again the question arises, what the alternative to payment is. Returning to CH, it may be questioned whether, in spite of the primary liability for multiple damages imposed upon the innocent purchaser, the alternative was death as in the case of the actual thief. The Babylonians were certainly aware that the purchaser's theft might be constructive only: in MVN 3,219 a merchant and his guarantor were said to have been "turned into" thieves when sheep the merchant had bought were "turned into" stolen sheep. Obviously the respectable merchant was the innocent purchaser of sheep subsequently found to be stolen. Nonetheless, he was obligated in damages, which his guarantor paid and then sought to recoup from the sellers. The

---

[56] *Theft*, p. 140.

[57] There is actually only one other occurrence, in Ex. 22,1.

[58] See AHw 1284-1285, (sub *šurqum*). Not all the examples given under meaning (b), 'Diebstahl', are unambiguous, but see especially the following, which establish the latter meaning beyond doubt:

1. AOAT 2 : the recurrent phrase in colophons *ša ina šurqi išarriqu / lu ina dannani ekimmu* "He who steals by theft or who takes away by force". 'By theft' here refers to the aspect of stealth. (See the references listed in the index on p. 175).

2. AbB 1,95,14 : *šurqam ina muhhika nadî* "...you are accused of theft". Cf. CH 1.

3. I Asb. 90,11 : ina *šurqi itbalamma* "he took it away from me by theft."

consequences of non-payment for the innocent merchant and his guarantor are unlikely to have been death.[59]

On the other hand, the codes do make a distinction between innocent and fraudulent possession. Persons who purchase goods in suspicious circumstances, especially from subordinate members of the family, are considered thieves and expressly liable to the death penalty (e.g. CH 7, AL 'A' 3). The distinction between innocent and fraudulent possession likewise seems to lie behind the different penalties in CE 40 and 49.

CE 40 reads:

If a man has bought a slave, a slave woman, an ox or any other purchase, however much it be, and does not establish the seller - he is a thief.

The sanction is not given, but it can safely be said to be the same as in CH 10, which presents the identical case in more detail:

If the buyer does not bring the seller who sold it to him nor the witnesses in whose presence he bought it, while the owner of the lost property brings the witnesses who know his lost property, the buyer is a thief. He shall be put to death. The owner of the lost property shall take his property.

If the buyer is unable to show innocent purchase, therefore, he is a real, not a constructive thief, and the penalty for theft will apply. As we have seen, this is in principle death, but according to the circumstances death will usually only be a residual penalty for failing to pay the fixed ransom. If the buyer can show innocent purchase, on the other hand, he is not relieved of liability to pay, but it is most likely a simple debt, leading at most to debt-slavery for non-payment.[60] CE 49 would appear to confirm this hypothesis:

If a man is seized with a stolen slave or a stolen slave woman, slave shall lead slave, slave woman shall lead slave woman.

Here, the possessor is not branded a thief, but the circumstances differ from CE 40 only in the failure to suggest any fraudulence in the possession. Yaron interprets the final phrase as meaning the

[59] See Westbrook and Wilcke, op. cit. note 16 above, 114-115.

[60] The difference in the ultimate penalties for innocent and fraudulent possession would explain three cases with which we had difficulty in the article cited at note 16 above (p.116). In Falkenstein (1956) vol. 2, no. 127, Sollberger (1976) p. 447 no. 10 and Goetze (1958) no. 28, the purchaser seeks to prove as his defence that he bought the stolen goods from a named seller. If by this tactic he could avoid the penalty altogether (as we suggested, ibid. p. 118), it would contradict the principle of strict liability established in the law codes. This contradiction disappears if the purpose of the buyer's tactic is not to avoid liability altogether but to reduce his penalty to that of a constructive thief, i.e. (lower) damages deemed a simple debt, rather than that of a real thief, i.e. damages with death for non-payment.

obligation to hand over a further slave or slave woman,[61] which would put the case on a par with the two-fold restitution demanded of an innocent possesor in HL. Certainly, the much lower level of payment required of an innocent possessor in CE, CH, HL and Ex. 22,3 makes it easier to posit a less severe penalty than death in case of non-payment.

In the result, it can be seen that the three theft provisions of Ex. 21,37 - 22,3 are arranged in descending order of severity: (a) the ordinary thief, for whom the penalty is a fixed ransom in the form of multiple damages in lieu of death; (b) the attempted burglar, for whom the penalty is an unlimited ransom in lieu of slavery: (c) the innocent possessor, for whom the penalty is a fixed ransom in the form of multiple damages in lieu of slavery.

To summarize, the law in Ex. 21,37 ff. draws together two traditional problems found in the ancient Near Eastern law codes: the three-cornered situation of owner, thief/seller and purchaser, and the case of attempted burglary. So far from being interpolated or disorganized, it uses them as the basis for a most orderly and logical presentation of the law of theft.

EXCURSUS: THE THEFT OF JOSEPH'S CUP

In Gen. 44,2 Joseph arranges for his cup to be planted in Benjamin's sack, so that the latter may be arrested for its theft. When accused of the crime, the unwitting brothers protest their innocence, adding: "With whomever of your servants it be found, let him die, and we also will be my lord's slaves" (v.9). Joseph's steward replies: "Let it be as you say: he with whom it is found shall be my slave, and the rest of you shall be blameless" (v.10).

As a source of the law of theft, the passage is fraught with difficulties. Two different penalties are proposed, death and slavery, and it is not clear which of them represents the law. If the brothers' statement is to be effective, it cannot be considered mere hyperbole.[62] But if it represents the law for theft, then two questions arise: why the death penalty was applicable in this case, and how it is that the steward could substitute a different penalty.

Jackson[63] regards the death penalty as applicable here because the stolen cup was a sacred article - we are informed in v. 5 that it was used by Joseph for divination. Although this is a possible interpretation, there are lacking the aggravating factors that

---

[61] *Eshnunna*, p. 172.

[62] As argued by Phillips, *loc. cit* note 47 above. On this point, see the perceptive remarks of Jackson, *Theft*, p. 166.

[63] *Ibid.*

mark the parallel examples: the theft of Laban's idol or of temple property in Babylonian law. In particular, it is clear from the information about the cup in v.5 that the brothers do not know, nor could be expected to know, about the cup's sacred properties, or even the identity of its owner.

Daube[64] sees the aggravating factor in the hot pursuit and formal search, as in the story of Jacob and Laban. Again, this is a possible interpretation, but it raises the second question: why is the sentence in fact reduced to slavery by the steward's words? Daube is troubled by this point, and concludes that the story is an ingenious but clumsy combination of different legal traditions.[65]

Commentators have tended to see the steward's words as an act of mercy reducing the sentence,[66] but this requires departure from the words of the text, which appear to state that the steward accepts the brothers' self- pronounced sentence.[67] Furthermore, one might ask how it is that the steward has the right to reduce a sentence or how he can do so before the question of guilt has even been determined.[68] We have postponed discussion of this case to an excursus because we consider that the solution to its difficulties does not lie in the sphere of the cuneiform legal tradition with which we have so far been concerned. In our view this narrative is a rare example of the application of Egyptian law in the Bible, as befits its Egyptian milieu, and probably its origin.

A feature peculiar to Egyptian procedural law[69] is that witnesses propose their own punishment for perjury, in the form of an oath that such-and-such be done to them if they are lying. This sentence is then automatically applied by the court should they be found to have broken their oath.[70] Where the witness is also the accused in a criminal trial and his evidence is essentially as to his own innocence, the accused in effect sets his own punishment should he be found guilty of the crime.

---

[64] *Biblical Law*, 236-245.

[65] *Ibid.* p. 245.

[66] E.g. Rashi, *ad. loc.*

[67] Ehrlich (*Randglossen zur Hebraïschen Bibel*, Leipzig 1980, *ad. loc.*) attempts to interpret the clause as concessive (as does the JPS), but this is based on his understanding of the content, not on any grammatical considerations.

[68] Nor, we would add, is such a concession psychologically appropriate to the story. The steward is supposed to be feigning outrage at the enormity of the brothers' crime.

[69] "Lurje has pointed out that the acknowledgement of penalties in judicial oaths is a point of contrast between Egyptian court procedure and that of contemporary Near Eastern cultures: see *Altägypt. Recht*, 144". Quoted by D. Lorton "Treatment of Criminals in Ancient Egypt" *JESHO* 20(1977) p32. Unfortunately, the original was not available to us.

[70] See J.A. Wilson, "The Oath in Ancient Egypt" *JNES* 7 (1948) 129-156 at 136-140, Examples 46-62 under the rubric 'An assertion of truth under penalty'.

Accordingly, punishment for the same crime can vary, since the accused may seek to convince the court of his innocence by proposing a heavier sentence. In the trials of tomb robbers, for example, the usual oath is: "If I speak falsehood, may I be mutilated and sent to Kush". But some suspected robbers invoke mutilation and impalement and some impalement only.[71]

This procedure is incompatible with the revenge and ransom system of cuneiform law, where discretion as to punishment lies primarily with the victim, and although subject to regulation by law, never passes into the hands of the perpetrator himself.

So ingrained was the concept of self-imposed punishment in Egyptian thought that it also became a literary motif. The story of Truth and Falsehood reveals how Truth's son uses this concept to gain revenge for his father.[72]

Falsehood, by deceitful methods,[73] has had Truth blinded and made his doorkeeper as the sentence of the court. Not content with this, he seeks to have Truth killed but unbeknownst to him, Truth is saved by loyal servants.

Truth's son now seeks revenge. By a stratagem, he manages to bring charges against Falsehood,[74] to turn the trial into a retrial of his father's case, and to bring the court to impose the following oath on Falsehood in order for him to establish his innocence: "By the life of Amon and by the life of the sovereign, if Truth is found alive, may I be blinded and made a doorkeeper in Truth's house!"

At this point the son triumphantly produces his father alive before the court. Falsehood receives his punishment: he is given a hundred blows and five wounds, blinded, and made a doorkeeper in Truth's house. And thus the son avenged his father.

The same literary motif derived from legal practice is, we suggest, behind the exchange between Joseph's brothers and the steward. Confident of their innocence, the brothers impose upon themselves a harsh penalty. This places the steward in a dilemma, since under Egyptian law their statement will be binding on the court and automatically condemn Benjamin to death. He therefore deliberately mishears them and purportedly accepts

---

[71] Lorton, *op. cit.* note 69 above, 32-36. According to Lorton (p.33): "One cannot, of course, suppose that the choice of penalty was at the discretion of the suspect, and so a more reasonable explanation must be sought for the observed discrepancy in the penalties mentioned... The simplest explanation .... is mere scribal confusion." With respect, it is the poorest explanation. The modern scholar who fails to account for an ancient phenomenon should not attribute his failure to the errors of the ancient scribes.

[72] Edited by A. Théodoridès, "Le Serment Terminal de 'Verité Mensonge'" *Revue d'Égyptologie* 21 (1969) 85-105, whose interpretation we follow here.

[73] He deposits a knife with Truth which for some reason the latter is unable to return.

[74] He deposits with Falsehood a bull which the latter seeks to keep for himself.

their proposed sentence, but in the milder form that is germane to Joseph's purposes. In vv. 16-17, when the brothers seek to accept joint responsibility for the crime, so as not to leave Benjamin alone, Joseph pretends to be horrified at the thought of not applying the procedural rule strictly: only Benjamin is to be enslaved and the rest can go free, in accordance with their proposal as "understood" by Joseph's steward.[75]

[75] For a preliminary discussion of our hypothesis, see S.I. Groll, *Pharaonic Egypt, the Bible and Christianity*, Jerusalem 1985, 374- 376.

CONCLUSIONS

Our study began with two premises: firstly, that Ancient Near Eastern Law, including that of the Bible, was based upon different concepts from those of modern law; secondly, that biblical law was based upon the same concepts as those of the other Ancient Near Eastern legal systems. We may now re-state our position in the light of the evidence adduced.

Ancient Near Eastern and Modern Law

As in modern systems, the machinery of justice in the Ancient Near East functioned to determine on the evidence whether a party had been wronged and, if necessary, to assist him by coercive means to obtain the appropriate remedy. From this point the systems begin to diverge:

1. Vital to a person's legal standing was his status within the family or clan. The role of the family was as important to determining the interested parties to a case as the events themselves. Thus we have seen that the plaintiff may be not the victim himself but a father, husband or slave-owner, or a brother or son (if the victim were deceased). In the same way, execution might fall not upon the wrongdoer himself, but upon another member of his family. Moreover, familial status could change the very extent of liability and its consequences, as for example where the victim was a pregnant wife, daughter or slave.

2. The principal interests protected by the law were the same as in modern law: property, contractual expectations, corporal integrity and honour. But there is little correlation between their approach to physical impingement upon property or person. The modern law seeks to protect what it perceives to be a public interest by means of the criminal law, while at the same time confining protection of the victim's interest to a right to pecuniary indemnity through the law of torts. The same wrongs in the ancient law gave rise to a dual right unknown to, and throughly repudiated by, modern systems: revenge or ransom (i.e. payment for foregoing revenge). The courts saw their role as setting the limits on both, in accordance with the circumstances of the case, and enabling execution. We have tried to show how the law codes attempted to

expound the principles upon which the courts were to exercise this role in the individual case.

3. The question of public interest was not ignored, however. Firstly, we have seen that responsibility was imposed upon the public authorities for the suppression of brigandage and for the maintenance of peace and good order in public places. Failure to do so led to a duty to compensate the victims from the public purse, a remedy only haltingly followed by modern systems. Secondly, the concept of "pollution" led to the intervention of the public authorities to prevent divine anger and the general calamity to the community that it would bring. The effect may have been in some instances like that of modern criminal law, but the theoretical basis was entirely different. Thus the polluting act might well be victimless, as with forbidden sexual acts, and the remedial action might affect unwitting persons who had become polluted only by association, such as the family of the culprit or the town in which he lived. The analogy is less to modern criminal law than to the treatment of a contagious disease.

4. At the head of the court system stood the King, but not simply in the manner of a modern court of appeal. He also had a discretionary authority to act entirely outside the system when it failed to do justice, whether through corruption, ineffectiveness or the harshness of the legal rules themselves.

Biblical and Cuneiform Law

We have seen in the course of these studies that all the concepts summarised above - revenge, ransom, vicarious liability, the public authorities' responsibility, pollution, the extra-judicial role of the king - existed in biblical law no less than in the cuneiform systems. The proof lies in the examples discussed, such as the theft provisions, where it is through the assumption of a common tradition that the texts, both biblical and cuneiform, emerge as a coherent, logical pattern of rules. Other explanations are forced to subject the texts to various kinds of surgery or to attribute to the ancient author (or putative redactor) incompetence in matters legal.

The real difference between biblical and cuneiform law lies in the fact that the Bible is a different kind of source. In particular, unlike the cuneiform texts, it contains the voice of dissent as much, if not more, than that of the establishment.

Thus the Mesopotamian kings praise themselves for having fulfilled their constitutional role of tempering with equity the oppressive effect of harsh laws, while the biblical sources accuse the Israelite kings of having failed to perform this very duty. Of the biblical law codes, the Covenant Code is the closest to the establishment and to presenting what might be regarded as the common law of Ancient Israel. The Priestly and Deuteronomic Codes, by contrast, are remarkable for their opposition to certain aspects of the common law, such as ransom and vicarious liability. But these two sources still work within the same conceptual framework, attempting to change the law by altering the field of application of some of the existing concepts to the detriment of others. Thus, as we have seen, the Priestly Code applies to the law of murder concepts of pollution familiar from the sphere of forbidden sexual relations.

What emerges from these studies then, apart from the re-interpretation of individual texts, is that biblical law is neither a mass of internal contradictions nor a monolith, but reflects a single, coherent common law, upon which different opinions were expressed. These opinions coincide, not surprisingly, with the major sources identified by modern biblical criticism.

BIBLIOGRAPHY

Al-Rawi, F.N.H. "Assult and Battery", Sumer 38 (1982) 117-120.

Ben-Haim, Z. "whw' šphh nḥrpt l'yš". Leshonenu 7 (5696) 362-366 (in Hebrew).

Boling, R. Judges. Anchor Bible, New York 1975.

Bottéro, J. "Le 'Code' de Hammurabi", Annali della Scuola Normale Superiore de Pisa 12 (1982) 409-444.

Bronznick, N.M. "Two Unrecognized Cases of *Talḥin*", Studies in Judaica, Karaitica and Islamica, presented to Dr. Leon Nemoy, Bar-Ilan 1982, 39- 45.

Büchler, A. Studies in Sin and Atonement in the Rabbinic Literature of the First Century, London 1928.

Buss, M. "The Distinction between Civil and Criminal Law in Ancient Israel", Proceedings of the 6th World Congress of Jewish Studies 1973, Vol.I (1977) 51-62.

Cardascia, G. "La Transmission des sources juridiques cunéiformes", Revue Internationale des Droits de l'Antiquité, 7 (1960) 43-50.

_____ Les Lois Assyriennes, Paris 1969.

_____ "Le Caractère Volontaire ou Involontaire des Atteintes Corporelles dans les Droits Cunéiformes", Studi in Onori di Cesare Sanfilippo Vol.6, Milan 1985, 163-207.

Cassuto, U. A Commentary on the Book of Exodus, Jerusalem 1967 (English translation).

Cazelles, H. Le Code de l'Alliance, Paris 1946.

Civil, M. "New Sumerian Law Fragments", Assyriological Studies 16 (Studies in Honour of B. Landsberger) 1965, 1-12.

Daube, D. Studies in Biblical Law, Cambridge 1947.
_____ ."Direct and Indirect Causation in Biblical Law", Vetus Testamentum 11 (1961) 246-269.

_____ ."Nathan's Parable", Novum Testamentum 24 (1982) 275-288.

Diamond, A.S. "An Eye for an Eye", Iraq 19 (1957) 151-155.

Driver, G.R. "Studies in the Vocabulary of the Old Testament III", Journal of Theological Studies 32 (1931) 361-365.

Driver, G.R. and J.C. Miles, The Assyrian Laws, Oxford 1935.
_____ . The Babylonian Laws, Pt.I, Oxford 1952; Pt.II, Oxford 1955.

Falk, Z.W. "Hebrew Legal Terms II", Journal of Semitic Studies 12 (1967) 241-244.

Fensham, F.C. "Widow, Orphan and the Poor in Ancient Near Eastern Legal and Wisdom Literature", Journal of Near Eastern Studies 21 (1962) 129-139.

Finkelstein, J.J. "Ammiṣaduqa's Edict and the Babylonian 'Law Codes'", Journal of Cuneiform Studies 15 (1961) 91-104.
_____ . "Some New Misharum Material and its Implications", Assyriological Studies 16 (Studies in Honour of B.Landsberger) 1965, 233-251.

_____ . "The Laws of Ur-Nammu", Journal of Cuneiform Studies 22 (1969) 66- 82.

_____ . The Ox That Gored, Transactions of the American Philosophical Society, Vol.71, Pt.2, 1981.

Forsthoff, E. Lehrbuch des Verwaltungsrechts, Vol.I, Munich 1973.

Frankena, R. Altbabylonische Briefe, Part II, Leiden 1966.

Friedrich, J. Die Hethitischen Gesetze, Leiden 1959.

Frymer-Kensky, T. "Tit for Tat", Biblical Archaeologist 43 (1980) 230-234.
_____ . "Pollution, Purification and Purgation in Biblical Israel",

Essays in Honour of D.N. Freedman, Philadelphia 1983, 399-414.

Geller, M.J. "The Šurpu Incantations and Lev.V 1-5", Journal of Semitic Studies 25 (1980) 181-192.

Goetze, A. The Laws of Eshnunna, Annual of the American Schools of Oriental Research 31, 1951-1952.

Gordis, R. "'Na' lam' and other Observations on the Ain Faška Scrolls", Journal of Near Eastern Studies 9 (1950) 44-47.

Greenberg, M. "Some Postulates of Biblical Criminal Law", Yehezkel Kaufmann Jubilee Volume, Jerusalem 1960, 5-28.

Greenfield, J.C. Našû - nadānu and its Congeners", Essays on the Ancient Near East in Memory of Jacob Joel Finkelstein, Memoirs of the Connecticut Academy of Arts and Sciences, Vol. XIX 1977, 87-91.

Groll, S.I. (ed.) Pharaonic Egypt, The Bible and Christianity, Jerusalem 1985.

Haase, R. "Regelt § 9 der hethitischen Rechtssammlung eine leichte Leibesverletzung?", Bibliotheca Orientalis 19 (1962) 114-116.
_____ . "Zur Tötung eines Kaufmanns nach den Hethitischen Gesetzen", Welt des Orients 9 (1977-1978) 217-219.

Hallo, W.W. and H.Tadmor "A Lawsuit from Hazor", Israel Exploration Journal 27 (1977) 1-11.

Hoffman, I. Der Erlass Telipinus, Heidelberg 1964.

Hoffner, H. The Laws of the Hittites (Diss. unpubl.), University Microfilm, Ann Arbor, 1963.
_____ . "Incest, Sodomy and Bestiality in the Ancient Near East", Alter Orient and Altes Testament 22 (1973) 81-90.

Jackson, B. Theft in Early Jewish Law, Oxford 1972.
_____ . Essays in Jewish and Comparative Legal History, Studies in Judaism in Late Antiquity X, Leiden 1975.

Jackson, B.S. and T.F. Watkins, "Distraint in the Laws of Eshnunna and Hammurabi", Studi in Onore di Cesare Sanfilippo Vol.5, Milan 1984, 411- 419.

Jacobson, T. An Ancient Mesopotamian Trial for Homicide, (in) Toward the Image of Tammuz, Harvard Semitic Series Vol.21, Cambridge, Mass. 1970, 193-214.

_____ . "Inūma ilu awīlum", Essays on the Ancient Near East in Memory of Jacob Joel Finkelstein, Memoirs of the Conneticut Academy of Arts and Sciences, 19 (1977) 113-117.

_____ . The Harab Myth, Sources from the Ancient Near East, Vol.2 Fasc.3, Malibu 1984.

Jolowicz, H.F. Historical Introduction to the Study of Roman Law, Cambridge 1952.

King, L.W. Babylonian Boundary-Stones and Memoral-Tablets in the British Museum, London 1912.

Klengel, H. "Mord und Busseleistung in spätbronzezeitlichen Syrien", (in) Death in Mesopotamia (ed. B. Alster) Copenhagen 1980.

Knudtzon, J.A. Die El-Amarna-Tafeln, Vorderasiatische Bibliothek, Vol.II Pt.1, Leipzig 1908.

Kohler, H. and A. Ungnad, Assyrische Rechtsurkunden, Leipzig 1913.

Korosec, V. "Le Problème de la Codification dans le Domaine du Droit Hittite", Revue Internationale des Droits de l'Antiquité 4 (1957) 93- 105.

Kraus, F.R. "Ein Zentrales Problem des altmesopotamischen Rechtes: Was ist der Codex Hammurabi?", Geneva 8 (1960) 283-296.

_____ . Vom mesopotamischen Menschen der altbabylonischen Zeit und seiner Welt, Amsterdam 1973.

_____ . Königliche Verfügungen in altbabylonischer Zeit, Studia et Documenta ad Iura Orientis Antiqui Pertinentia, XI, Leiden 1984.

Lambert, M. "Les 'reformes' d'Urukagina", Revue d'Assyriologie 50 (1956) 169-184.

Lambert, W.G. Babylonian Wisdom Literature, Oxford 1960.

Laubadère, A. de, Traité de Droit Administratif (8th ed.), Paris 1980.

Lauterbach, J.Z. Mekilta de-Rabbi Ishmael, Philadelphia 1935.

Leemans, W.F. "Some Aspects of Theft and Robbery in Old-Babylonian Documents", Rivista degli Studi Orientali 32 (1957) 661-666.

Lemche, N.P. "The Hebrew Slave", Vetus Testamentum 25 (1975) 136-144.

Lifshitz, B. "Does a Man Not Receive Both the Death Penalty and Pay Damages?", (On the Question of the Origin of the Rule "Kam leh Miderabah Mineh"), Shenaton Ha-Mishpat Ha-Ivri 8 (1981) 153-246 (in Hebrew).

Loewenstamm, S. Review of Goetze's "Laws of Eshunna", Israeli Exploration Journal 7 (1957) 192-198.
____ . "The Laws of Adultery and Murder in Biblical and Mesopotamian Law", Alter Orient und Altes Testament 204 (1980) 146-153.

____ . "bqrt thyh", Shnaton 4 (1980) 94-97 (in Hebrew).

Lorton, D. "The Treatment of Criminals in Ancient Egypt", Journal of the Economic and Social History of the Orient 20 (1977) 2-64.

Maag, V. "Erwägungen zur Deuteronomischen Kultzentralisation", Vetus Testamentum 6 (1956) 10-18.

McKeating, H. "The Development of the Law on Homicide in Ancient Israel", Vetus Testamentum 25 (1975) 46-68.

Mendenhall, G. The Tenth Generation, Baltimore 1973.

Milgrom, J. Cult and Conscience, Studies in Judaism in Late Antiquity XVIII, Leiden 1976.
____ . "The Bethrothed Slave-Girl, Lev. 19, 20-22", Zeitschrift für Alttestamentische Wissenschaft 89 (1977) 43-50.

Muffs, J. Studies in the Aramaic Legal Papyri from Elephantine. Studia et Documenta ad Iura Orientis Antiqui Pertinentia, VIII, Leiden 1969.

Müller, D.H. Die Gesetze Hammurabis, Vienna 1903.

Naveh, J. "A Hebrew Letter from the Seventh Century B.C.", Israel Exploration Journal 10 (1960) 129-139.

Neu, E. Althethitische Ritualtexte in Umschrift, Studien zu den Bogasköy- Texten 25 (1980), 26 (1983).

Noth, M. Exodus (Engl. transl.) Old Testament Library, Philadelphia 1959.

Nougayrol, J. Le Palais Royal d'Ugarit IV (=Mission de Ras Shamra IX) Paris, 1956.

Oppenheim, A.L. Ancient Mesopotamia, Chicago 1964.

Paul, S. Studies in the Book of the Covenant in the Light of Cuneiform and Biblical Law, Vetus Testamentum Supplement 18, Leiden 1970.

Phillips, A. "The Interpretation of 2 Samuel xii 5-6", Vetus Testamentum 16 (1966) 242-244.
_____ . Ancient Israel's Criminal Law, Oxford 1970.

_____ . "Another Look at Murder", Journal of Jewish Studies 28 (1977) 105- 126.

Pitard, W.T. "Amarna *ekēmu* and Hebrew *nāqam*", Maariv 3 (1982) 5-25.

Postgate, J.N. Fifty Neo-Assyrian Legal Documents, Warminster 1976.

Prévost, H. "L'oppression dans la Bible", Mélanges Prévost, Paris 1982, 3-16.

Prosser, W.L. Law of Torts (4th ed.) St.Paul, Minnesota 1971.

Reiner, E. Surpu, Archiv für Orientforschung, Beiheft 11, Graz 1958.

Riccobono, S. Fontes Iuris Romani Anteiustiniani, Pt.I, Florence 1941.
Rofé, A. "The History of the Cities of Refuge in Biblical Law", Scripta Hierosolymitana 31 (Jerusalem 1986) 205-239.

San Nicolò, M. Die Schlussklauseln der altbabylonischen Kauf - und Tauschverträge, Munich 1922.
Schooeveld, J. "Le Sang du Cambrioleur - Ex 22: 1-2", Symbolae de Liagre Böhl, Leiden 1973, 335-340.

Schuler, E. von, Hethitische Dienstanweisungen, Archiv fu@"r Orientforschung, Beiheft 10, Graz 1957.

Schwartz, B.J. "A Literary Study of the Slave-Girl Pericope - Leviticus 19: 20-22", Scripta Hierosolymitana 31 (Jerusalem 1986) 241-255.

Scott, R.B.Y. Proverbs/Ecclesiastes, Anchor Bible, New York 1965.

Seebass, H. "Nathan und David in II Sam 12", Zeitschrift fu@"r die Alttestamentliche Wissenschaft 86 (1974) 203-211.

Segal, P. Liability under Divine Jurisdiction (Diss. unpubl.) - Hebrew University 1986.

Simon, UU "The Poor Man's Ewe-Lamb", Biblica 48 (1967) 207-242.

Smith, J.C. and B. Hogan Criminal Law (5th ed.) London 1983.

Soyer, J.C. Droit Pénale et Procédure Pénale (5th ed.) Paris 1977.

Speiser, E.A. "Leviticus and the Critics", Yehezkel Kaufmann Jubilee Volume, Jerusalem 1960, 29-45.

Szlechter, E. Les Lois d'Esnunna, Paris 1954.

Teixidor, J. Bulletin d'Epigraphie Sémitique, Syria 50 (1973) 416-417.

Théodoridès, A. "Le Serment Terminal de 'Verité-Mensonge'", Revue d'Egyptologie 21 (1969) 85-105.

Van der Ploeg, J.M.P. Slavery in the Old Testament, Vetus Testamentum Supplement 22, Leiden 1971.

Van Selms, A. "The Best Man and Bride - From Sumer to St. John", Journal of Near East Studies 9 (1950) 65-75.
_____ . "The Goring Ox in Babylonian and Biblical Law", Archiv Orientalni 18/4 (1950) 328-330.

Vaux, R. de, Studies in Old Testament Sacrifice, Cardiff 1964.

Wade, H.W.R. Administrative Law (5th ed.) Oxford 1982.
Weinfeld, M. Deuteronomy and the Deuteronomic School, Oxford 1972.

_____ . Justice and Righteousness in Israel and the Nations,

Jerusalem 1985 (in Hebrew).

Wenham, G. The Book of Leviticus, New International Commentary on the Old Testament, Grand Rapids 1979.

Westbrook, R. "Purchase of the Cave of Machpelah", Israel Law Review 6 (1971) 29-38.
_____ . "Redemption of Land", Israel Law Review 6 (1971) 367-375.

_____ .. "The Biblical Law of Levirate", Revue Internationale des Droits de l'Antiquité 24 (1977) 65-87.

_____ . "Biblical and Cuneiform Law Codes", Revue Biblique 92 (1985) 247- 264.

_____ . "Lex Talionis and Exodus 21, 22-25", Revue Biblique 93 (1986) 52- 69.

_____ . Old Babylonian Marriage Law, Archiv für Orientforschung Beiheft 23 (forthcoming).

Westbrook, R. and C. Wilke "The Liability of an Innocent Purchaser of Stolen Goods in Early Mesopotamian Law", Archiv für Orientforschung 25 (1974-1977) 111-121.

Whitelam, K.W. The Just King, Journal for the Study of the Old Testament, Supplement 12, Sheffield 1979.

Wilson, J.A. "The Oath in Ancient Egypt", Journal of Near Eastern Studies 7 (1948) 129-156.

Yaron, R. The Laws of Eshnunna, Jerusalem 1969.

Yildiz, F. "A Tablet of Codex Ur-Nammu from Sippar", Orientalia 50 (1981) 87-97.

Zakovitch, Y. The Life of Samson, Jerusalem 1982 (in Hebrew).

Zulueta, F. de, The Institutes of Gaius Pt.II, Oxford 1953.

INDEX OF SOURCES

B. CUNEIFORM LAW CODES

MVN 3
219   126-127

Nippur Murder Trial
                          47-49, 52, 78

PRU IV (Ugarit)
17.146   67
17.158   67
17.230   67
17.251   67
17.337   67

Sollberger
AOAT 25(1976)   p.443
10   127 n.60

Šurpu
                            28-29

Telipinus Edict
49   49-50

YBC 2177 (=YOS 1 28)
                            40, 62

D. RABBINIC SOURCES

Mishna Baba Qamma
15 n.25

Talmud B. Qiddushin
70a   106 n.74

Tosefta Baba Qamma
7.2   111 n.2

E. ROMAN LAW

Twelve Tables
8,2-3   40 n.8
8,2-4   41 n.18, 71-72

Gaius, Institutes

3.223   72

IMP. A. BONTEMPS, LIMOGES (France). - Dépôt légal : Mai 1988. - IMP. N° 23507-88